COLLECTING

MINIATURE COLOURED COTTAGES

New Cavendish Books

London

COLLECTING

MINIATURE COLOURED COTTAGES

A tour round the historic
cottages and buildings of Britain
through their china models

SAM AND MAGGIE SEABROOK

New Cavendish Books
London

Dedication

This book is dedicated to our friends and fellow collectors, Margaret and the late Roland Latham

First edition published in Great Britain in 1996 by
New Cavendish Books Ltd

Designed by Jacky Wedgwood
Edited by Narisa Chakra
Photography by the authors and Nick Nicholson
Typesetting by Bartlett Rice Associates, London

Printed and bound in Bangkok by
Eastern Printing (Public) Company

New Cavendish Books Ltd.
3 Denbigh Road
London W11 2SJ

ISBN 1 872727 972

Acknowledgments

We would like to thank the hundreds of people who helped us to compile this book in addition to those to whom we owe particular thanks listed below: Pamela Abraham, Anne Bonnett, Mrs S.P. de Burlet, Duncan Chilcott, Sheila and Alan Donelly, Mrs S. England, Ron Gough, Tom Hood, the Landmark Trust, Margaret and Roland Latham, Andrea McAfee of the Ballymoney Heritage Centre, Tony Mundy, Linda and Nicholas Pine, Robin and Philip Riley, John Rolls, Margaret Seabrook, Ted Stansmore, David Taylor, K. Temple-Smith, Kath and Graham Walder, Hilda Winter; the curators and trustees of the following museums and institutions: The Alloway Burns Monument Trustees; Church of Scotland; Parks and Recreation City of Glasgow; the Folklore Society (Glastonbury); The Trustees of Dove Cottage; Gretna Green Marriage Houses; The Manx Museum and National Trust, Douglas; Davestone Holdings Ltd (Lands End); Johnson Birthplace Museum; Borough of Poole Museum Service; Tudor House Museum, Southampton; the Portadown Times; Staffordshire County Museum; Shakespeare Birthplace Trust; The Sulgrave Manor Board; Malvern Hills District Council; A.H. Baldwin & Sons Ltd. (Pevensey); Royal Institute of Cornwall; Keith M. Thompson of Ruthin School; Barclays Bank, Ruthin; The Shakespeare Institute (Masons Croft). Thank you too for pictures from the Woolf Greenham Collection (Newquay); The Joint Management Committee, Cook's Cottage, Melbourne and Shropshire Libraries.

Authors technical note

We used Kodak film and a Nikormat 135 camera with 50mm and 28mm lenses and Ektachrome film with a close-up lens for the indoor pictures.

CONTENTS

FOREWORD 6

INTRODUCTION 7

PART I

COTTAGES BY GOSS 8

Company History
Notes for Collectors including Rarity Guide
Locations of Goss Cottages 12
A-Z of Goss Cottages 13

PART 2

COTTAGES BY OTHER MANUFACTURERS 61

Company Histories

Arcadian China, Willow Art and Willow China,
Podmore China, Swan China, Tuscan China, Carlton China,
Wilton China, Savoy China, Taylor & Kent, Grafton China,
Leadbeater Art China, Unidentified Potteries.

Locations of Cottages by Other Manufacturers 66
A-Z of Cottages by Other Manufacturers 69

MISCELLANEOUS BUILDINGS 125

INDEX 126

FOREWORD

My grandparents lived in the Potteries and my grandmother was an enthusiastic collector of ceramics. Her collection comprised the products of several Staffordshire factories and she was on friendly terms with many of the potters who ran the various concerns. She knew the Goss family and was particularly fond of their china models of various famous houses, churches and other buildings known collectively as 'cottages'.

In a family where fine china and porcelain was discussed, appreciated and always on display, it was perhaps inevitable that I too became a collector, although I have to admit my first contact with a Goss cottage ended in disaster. Apparently as a babe in arms I took a playful swipe at one of my grandmother's better pieces and smashed it to smithereens.

This type of incident apart, I cannot think of any other aspect of collecting that is anything less than thoroughly rewarding and enjoyable. The visual joy and the pride of having a collection is enormously rewarding as are the memories of people and places involved with a particular purchase. Certainly there is nothing to beat the thrill of the chase in tracking down a rarity, or perhaps stumbling across something special in some out of the way antique shop. Financial reward may also accrue but cannot be relied upon and, in my opinion, should never be a motive for collecting. As outlined above, there are rewards enough in other ways.

Happily, after William Henry Goss had introduced his delightful and accurate 'cottages' in the 1890s, other factories such as Willow Art, Grafton, Arcadian, Carlton etc. were to follow his idea with models of their own. In the manner of Goss, though never excelling him, they produced well finished pieces with good attention to detail which the relatively inexpensive labour costs of the day made possible. Only in the 1930s, after the great depression of the late 1920s had savaged the industry, does one sometimes notice a coarsening of the potting and painting but even these pieces have a certain robust charm. However, despite the not inconsiderable production of cottages, with some still being produced close to the outbreak of the Second World War, they are today extremely hard to locate and the serious collector has to be patient, highly mobile and in touch with a tolerant bank manager in order to succeed.

Maggie and Sam Seabrook have brilliantly combined their respective hobbies, Sam's as a collector and Maggie's as photographer, to produce this delightful book. It takes us into the charming world of ordinary people at the time of W H Goss and his fellow potters, and the 'cottages' they produced many years ago, together with an up-to-date view of things for comparison.

Philip Riley

INTRODUCTION

The late Victorian and early
20th century cottage industry

This title was suggested by Robin & Philip Riley and the word 'industry' is indeed appropriate, as many cottages – especially those of writers – were visited by hundreds of people annually and a china souvenir industry was created to meet the demands of these visitors. Many cottages still have the penciled price on the base - 1/3 or 2/9 etc (the equivalent of 6p or 14p today).

Today, these cottages represent a model of the past, a three-dimensional potter's record, which tells us the appearance of the historical buildings when the potter copied them.

Of course, there was no television or films at the turn of the century and the middle classes tended to read books avidly. Thus cottages with a literary connection such as those of Dickens, Thomas Hardy, Samuel Johnson, Barrie, Burns, Bunyan, Craik, Corelli, Walton, Wordsworth, and Shakespeare were perennial favourites, while those of other personalities like Ellen Terry and Lloyd George were also popular. Churches with special features were also visited, as well as such curiosities as 'The First and Last House' and 'The First and Last Post Office'. Other much visited buildings at that time included Sulgrave Manor, St Ives and those at Glastonbury .

We have visited all of the buildings copied by the model makers (or their sites), and decided that our 'Top Ten' cottages were first Burns' cottage at Ayr, then Sulgrave Manor, with Ledbury Market and The Priest's House, Prestbury next, followed by Dove Cottage and the Ostrich Inn at Colnbrook sixth. The two St Nicholas chapels are seventh and eighth.

Stokesay Castle Gatehouse was ninth whilst the Hop Kiln, Headcorn, just squeezed ahead of St Catherine's Chapel and Godalming's Pepper Pot at tenth. But in fact it was a difficult choice, as all had interesting features.

Fortunately most of the real life buildings which were copied so meticulously in miniature still exist, and many are·maintained in excellent condition – perhaps the best maintained one being Sulgrave Manor, the interior of which especially is a joy to behold. Of those that no longer exist, Bunyan's Cottage and the thatched cottages at Poole and Bournemouth (Portman Lodge) have been demolished as a result of commercial pressures. The Look-Out House at Newquay was demolished because it was no longer required and the Old Market Hall at Church Stretton was destroyed by fire in 1838. The Manx Cottage and Jean MacAlpine's Inn deteriorated quickly once they were left unused and the one entitled 'Joseph of Arimathoea' vanished centuries ago (if it ever existed).

We had a great deal of pleasure in finding out about all the cottages, discovering a secondary hobby in postcard collecting, as postcards proved an invaluable source of information for those buildings that no longer exist. In some cases we may have unearthed facts that may not be available in a few years time – particularly those relating to the Manx Cottage, The Look-Out House, Newquay, and The Hop Kiln at Headcorn. Altogether we have travelled some 30,000 miles, visiting many of the sites on two and sometimes three occasions as more information has come to light, or because better weather was needed for a photograph.

PART ONE
COTTAGES BY GOSS

History of W H Goss

As a large proportion of the cottages and ecclesiastical buildings discussed in this book were copied and produced by W H Goss at his pottery works, known as the 'Falcon Works,' in Stoke-on-Trent, a few details about William Henry Goss and his family may well be of interest.

William H Goss was born in 1833 in London and it is believed that he studied art at the Government School of Design at Somerset House. He learned the art of pottery and, becoming an efficient chemist under the guidance of Copeland, he eventually became their chief artist. Although very little is recorded about his work at this time, it is known that the so-called Shakespeare 'Night-light' with a separate base was produced by Copeland in 1847 and this may have had an influence on the young Goss. (In fact, this item was probably a novelty cigar rest in which the smoke went out through the chimney). It is believed that he designed an exquisite jewelled dessert service, bought by the Shah of Persia, which still exists intact in Tehran.

By 1857 his skill and taste as a designer were becoming well known.

After leaving Copeland's in 1858, Goss formed a partnership with a Mr Peake, although very little is known about this gentleman. During the period with Mr Peake, terracotta pieces were recorded, marked 'Goss and Peake', together with ornamented Parian ware and figures.

In 1859, he moved to his own works in London Road, Stoke-on-Trent where he stayed for 12 years (although some sources suggest that he moved to a pottery in Johns Street close to Copeland's works). The firm moved to the 'Falcon Works' some time between 1869-1872 and this was to be the home of the works for the next 60 years.

During these early years Goss produced a variety of wares, all of good quality, developing the well known ivory porcelain body, a form of glazed Parian. In 1862, he had been awarded a bronze medal for his exhibit of porcelain at the International Exhibition. In 1872 he patented several improvements to the manufacture of jewelled porcelain and was granted a patent for

*The Old
Falcon Works.*

'Improvements in manufacturing articles of jewellery, dress ornaments, dress-fastenings etc.'

In the 1880s manufacture of the more costly wares was gradually discontinued and replaced by products which had a wider appeal – the most important step being the production of heraldic souvenirs in ivory porcelain. Some heraldic china had been produced in Goss' earlier years but these were only for Cambridge, Oxford and various famous public schools. In those days very little was known about heraldry by the general public and Goss felt that so interesting a subject would be of general interest to all. Adolphus, Goss' eldest son, visited various parts of Britain making sketches of antique pottery and producing them in ivory porcelain with the arms of the town being placed on the piece, which would then only be available for purchase in that town with one agent (a policy later waived). This venture met with renowned success and other potteries followed in Goss's footsteps. Goss had over 500 agents appointed and over 100 shapes were being produced by the turn of the century. Goss was a keen antiquarian and a great enthusiast for heraldry, as was Adolphus his son.

It was in 1893 that Adolphus thought of producing miniature coloured models of interesting and well known buildings now called 'cottages'. They were perfectly modelled and accurately painted and are still a source of great pleasure to the collectors of Goss and cottages.

The first 'cottages' produced were large models intended as night-lights, with smaller varieties being produced when the night-lights proved to be successful. Models were still being prepared for production in 1921, although interest had waned considerably since their heyday before the First World War.

W H Goss died in 1906 leaving his son Adolphus £4,000 and the business to Victor Henry and William Huntley Goss. Adolphus appears to have had little to do with the business from that date.

The firm gradually declined from the time of W H Goss's death as the money (£4,000) had to be withdrawn from the firm and then in 1913 Victor Henry Goss was killed by being thrown from his horse.

The war, a year later, caused more difficulties with a shortage of labour and loss of export trade. Unfortunately the firm did not start producing 'war models' until the market had already been captured by other potteries. Goss also tried to produce dolls' heads, arms and legs as they could no longer be imported from Germany but this was not a successful venture.

After the war the firm's prosperity declined further, the changes in public taste and the economic situation being partly responsible, with the lack of money making it difficult to develop more profitable alternatives. In 1928 bankruptcy was imminent and the firm passed into the hands of Cauldon Potteries Ltd thus severing the connection with the Goss family which had endured for over seventy years.

The firm was known as W H Goss Ltd from 1930-1934 and then as the Goss China Company Ltd. The new firm used the trade name of W H Goss England to try to sell its inferior products, but few are very desirable. Production came to an end in 1940 when the site was used for storage purposes.

Messrs. Ridgway & Adderley purchased the Goss models, blocks and engravings from Coalport China Co. Ltd and the goodwill,

*This photo shows the differences between the Copeland cottage of 1847
(right), and the Goss, 1893, night-light and how the production of the Copeland
may have influenced Goss.*

patterns and trade marks from Goss China Co.
Ltd in 1954 – no further models have been
produced and it seems they are unlikely to be
made again.

Goss' first coloured cottage

In order to establish which was Goss' first
coloured cottage, we have made investigations by
going first to Stoke and the Spode Museum, and,
then by writing to the Victoria & Albert Museum
who replied almost by return.

At the Spode Museum we spoke to Robert
Copeland and studied their two-piece
Shakespeare's night-light which proved very easy
to date as it bore a Class IV registration mark,
indicating it was registered on 21st September
1847 (see photostat copy of base of cottage).
This shows that the cottage must have been
designed marginally before that date when
William Goss would only have been thirteen.

However, the cottage would have been about
when Goss was at Copelands and we believe
that its success must have influenced Goss' later
decision to produce a similar model.

Mr R J C Hildyard of the V & A has advised us
that the night-light had been registered by a
Egerton Jacobson Filmore of 1, Furnivals Inn,
Holborn, London, and was presumably made by
Copelands under licence.

The original illustration indicates that it was
"To be registered for three years in Class Four

in the name of Egerton Jacobson Filmore …"

(When one goes back into 'records' one
wonders just how often a name from the past
has come to light - in this case Mr Filmore may
not have surfaced for 100 years!)

Forgeries

These have occurred and may well do so again.
Thus models reputed to be by Goss but without
the markings must be treated with the greatest
suspicion. To be a genuine unmarked Goss they
must be very sharply defined and well made as
Goss was a supreme craftsman. They should also
be the same size and shape as given in the text. If
a forger has, or had, an original Goss piece in
order to construct a mould, the resulting model
would be substantially smaller because of the
reducing effect of firing. Models that are Goss
are all listed in this book, as Goss made records
of all his production plans. Only Plas Newydd,
Atlantic Hotel (Land's End) and the coloured
Massachusetts Hall have not yet been seen by us
or other collectors. Thus any cottage not
referred to in this book as Goss but bearing the
Goshawk mark is almost certainly a fabrication
of some sort.

We are aware of two fake Goss models.
Trefriw Wells (No 97) has had a Goshawk mark
applied later, while another model reputed to be
of St Nicholas Chapel in Ilfracombe has turned
out to be a model of Lullington Church (No. 80)

Rarity guide to coloured Goss and Goss England cottages

An Clachan (2)	A+	Gullane Smithy	B+	Manx Cottage (NL)	C+	Lloyd George with	
Holden Chapel	A+	Poole	B+	Wordsworth		annexe	D+
Toll Bar, Gretna Green	A+	John Knox	B+	Cockermouth	C+	Charles Dickens (2)	D+
Hop Kiln	A+	St Catherine's Chapel	B+	Burns (NL)	C	Window in Thrums	D+
Sulgrave Manor	A+	Thomas Hardy	B	First and Last (NL)	C	Old Maids, Lee	D
Priest's House,		Portman Lodge (2)	B	Ann Hathaway (NL)	C	Newquay Look-Out (2)	D
Presbury	A	Ellen Terry	B	Shakespeare (NL)	C	Manx cottage	D
Bunyan's Cottage	A	Dove Cottage	B	St Nicholas Chapel		Huer's House	D
Izaak Walton (large)	A	Ledbury Market House	B-	Ilfracombe	C-	Prince Llewelyn	D
Arimathoea	A	Old Court House	B-	St Nicholas Chapel		First and Last without	
First and Last with		Southampton,		St Ives	C-	annexe	D-
Annex	A-	Tudor House	B-	Lloyd George without		Burns	D-
Feathers Hotel	A-	Window in Thrums		annexe	C-	Hathaway	D-
Izaak Walton (small)	A-	(NL)	B-	First and Last Post		Shakespeare (variations)	
Abbot's Kitchen (2)	A-	Cat & Fiddle, Buxton	C+	Office	C-		D-t
		Goss Oven (2)	C+	Samuel Johnson	D+		D+

Notes: A+ = extremely rare D- = most numerous NL = Night-light. Examples of Plas Newydd and coloured Massachusetts Hall have not come to light, although shards of the latter have been found; if an example is found it would be A+

with a Goshawk and early registration mark affixed. As mentioned earlier, Goss took great care to get accurate proportions and details. However, in these particular models there are significant differences.

Registration numbers

Up until the First World War, all cottages designed by Goss were registered or patented and given a number. Although the registration number was only legally valid for four years, Goss continued to use them throughout the production run. Below is a list of registration numbers and the date of first registration. Where variations exist for a particular cottage such as the First and Last House, all versions bear the same number.

208047 Ann Hathaway's Cottage 1893
211037 Burns Cottage 1893
225833 Shakespeare's House 1894
273243 Manx Cottage 1896
322142 A Window in Thrums 1898
521645 First and Last House 1908
594374 Prince Llewelyn's House 1912
602905 St Nicholas Chapel, St Ives 1912
605733 Samuel Johnson's House 1912
605735 Look-Out House, Newquay 1912
610011 Huer's House, Newquay 1912
613770 St Nicholas Chapel, Ilfracombe 1913
617573 Lloyd George's House 1913
618950 First and Last Post Office 1913
622406 Old Maids' Cottage, Lee 1913
630367 Charles Dickens' House 1914

638372 Sulgrave Manor 1914
639535 Wordsworth's House 1914
641313 Ellen Terry's Farm 1914
643867 Holden Chapel 1914
647235 Massachusetts Hall 1914

Copyright

All the other Goss Cottages were produced after the First World War and the majority have the word 'Copyright' printed on them.

The value of cottages

The most numerous cottages such as Shakespeare's and Ann Hathaway's cottages are among the cheapest, whilst the rarest, such as the Old Toll Bar, Gretna Green and the Hop Kiln, Headcorn, are among the most expensive. The most expensive Goss items can cost 30 to 50 times as much as the least expensive (rarity alone is not the governing factor as appeal is also to be considered – cottages that are not pretty are not wanted by some collectors).

Above we give an indication of the rarity of the Goss cottages. So little is known about the non-Goss cottages that estimating their value is more difficult. They are often very hard to find and may be very expensive in a few years when more is known of them, despite the fact that they are usually less well made than the Goss. Nevertheless a similar rarity guide may be found at the beginning of the section on cottages by other makers (see page 68).

GOSS COTTAGE LOCATIONS (These refer to the numbers on the map)

● Existing Goss cottages ● Site of cottages modelled by Goss which no longer exist ○ Cottages by other manufacturers * Site of cottages by other manufacturers no longer existing

1 *Abbotsbury, Dorset*
St Catherines Chapel

2 *Ayr, Scotland*
Burns Cottage (Alloway)

3 *Beddgelert, Wales*
Prince Llewellyns House

4 *Bedford*
Bunyans Cottage
(Elstow)

5 *Boston, USA*
Holden Chapel
(Not shown on map)

6 *Boston, USA*
Massachusetts Hall
(Not shown on map)

7 *Bournemouth*
Portman Lodge

8 *Buxton, Derbyshire*
The Cat & Fiddle Inn

9 *Christchurch, Hampshire*
The Old Court House

10 *Cockermouth, Cumbria*
Wordsworth's
Birthplace

11 *Criccieth, Gwynedd
Wales*
Lloyd Georges Early
Home,
(Llanystumdwy)

12 *Dorchester, Dorset*
Thomas Hardy's
Birthplace
(HigherBockhampton)

13 *Edinburgh, Scotland*
John Knox's House

14 *Glasgow, 1938 Empire
Exhibition,*
An Clachan

15 *Glastonbury Abbey
Somerset*
The Abbott's Kitchen

16 *Glastonbury, Somerset*
Church of Arimathoea

17 *Grasmere, Cumbria*
Wordsworth's Home
Dove Cottage

18 *Gretna Green, Scotland*
Old Toll Bar

19 *Gullane, Lothian
Scotland*
Gullane Smithy

20 *Headcorn, Kent*
Hop Kiln

21 *Ilfracombe, Devon*
Old Maids Cottage
(Lee)

22 *Ilfracombe, Devon*
St Nicholas Chapel

23 *Isle of Man*
Manx Cottage

24 *Kirriemuir, Tayside
Scotland*
A Window in Thrums

25 *Lands End, Cornwall*
First and Last House
in England

26 *Ledbury, Herefordshire*
Feathers Hotel

27 *Ledbury, Herefordshire*
Old Market House

28 *Lichfield, Staffordshire*
Samuel Johnson's
Birthplace

29 *Llangollen, Clwyd, Wales*
Plas Newydd

30 *Newquay, Cornwall*
Huers House

31 *Newquay, Cornwall*
Look-Out House

32 *Poole, Dorset*
Old Thatched Cottage

33 *Prestbury, Cheshire*
Priests House

34 *Rochester, Kent*
Dickens' House

35 *St Ives, Cornwall*
St Nicholas Chapel

36 *Sennen, Cornwall*
First and Last
Post Office

37 *Shallowford, Staffs*
Izaak Walton's
Birthplace

38 *Southampton*
Tudor House

39 *Stoke-on-Trent*
Goss Oven

40 *Stratford-on-Avon
Warwickshire*
Ann Hathaway's
Cottage (Shottery)

41 *Stratford-on-Avon
Warwickshire*
Shakespeare's
Birthplace

42 *Sulgrave
Northamptonshire*
Sulgrave Manor

43 *Tenterden, Kent*
Ellen Terry's
Farmhouse

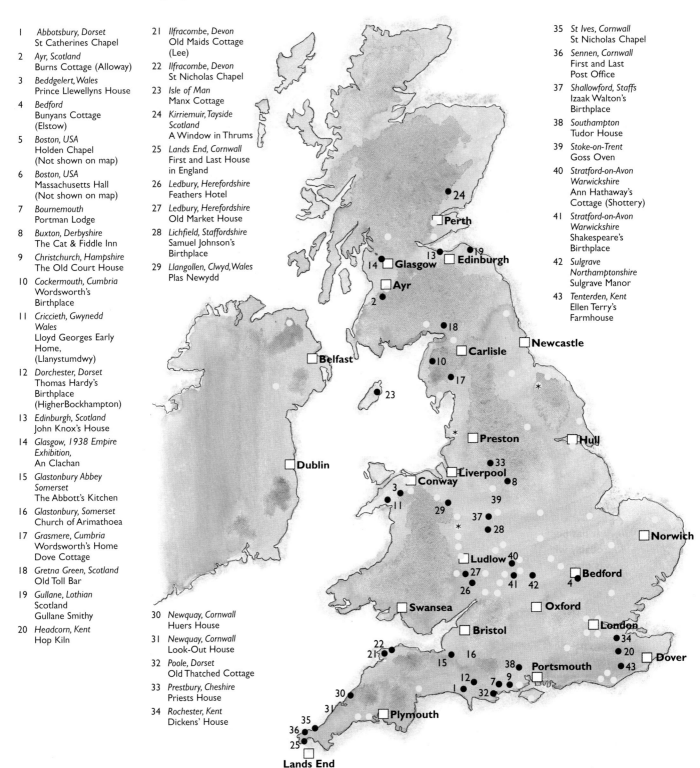

ABBOTSBURY, DORSET

1 St Catherine's Chapel

The chapel which belonged originally to the Benedictine Abbey of Abbotsbury and was probably built in the fourteenth century, stands at the top of a hill dominating a strip of the Dorset coastline. It is a fine example of a chapel dedicated to the cult of St Catherine.

The abbey, including its vast grounds, was leased to Sir Giles Strangeways in 1539 after the dissolution of the monasteries, on condition that "all edifices being within the site and precinct ... be hereafter thrown down and removed". Most of the stonework of the old abbey and monastery was used by the villagers to build their own houses. The chapel escaped this vandalism probably because it was a fair distance away.

It has been retained ever since as a seamark, which is probably why repairs were undertaken on it in 1742. It was placed in the guardianship of H M Office of Works in 1922. The entire area, including the famous swannery and the village of Abbotsbury itself, has been kept to extremely high standards owned as it is by one family.

The chapel, which is considered to have unusual external elevations, is constructed of local stone and the roof was recently repaired, using the same material. Inside, in the northwest corner, a newel stair has been rebuilt in wood. This leads to the roof and to a tiny

chapel in the head of the stair turret, where there remains one of a pair of ancient stone supports for its altar slab. It has an ornate ceiling, partly reconstructed, supported by a central column with a richly carved capital.

The main chapel has a warm feeling about it, despite its earthen floor and bare stone walls. The outside, particularly where it faces seaward is becoming worn by the elements.

St. Catherine, who is commemorated on 15 November, was a high born and scholarly maiden lady of the city of Alexandria. During the persecutions of Emperor Maximes Daza, she was tortured on the wheel and then beheaded in AD 310. She was widely venerated during the middle ages as the patron saint both of philosophers and of spinsters. Women in search of a husband prayed to her:

"A Husband, St Catherine
A Handsome One, St Catherine
A Rich One, St Catherine
A Nice One, St Catherine
And Soon, St Catherine"

This unusual model measures 8.7cm long, 5.4cm deep and 6.1cm high.

AYR, SCOTLAND

2 Burns Cottage (Alloway)

Robert Burns, the great Scottish poet, was born in this cottage at Alloway, Ayr on the first Burns night 25 January 1759.

The family though very poor were none-the-less hard working and far sighted. Hard working because his father built the cottage himself in the 1750s using clay and thatch before white-washing the dry walls; far sighted because his parents insisted that the sons amongst their seven children were well educated and able to read. Before that time Robert's mother taught her children the many songs which were to become the foundation of his famous works. When Robert was seven years old the family moved a mile away to rent a small farm but retained the ownership of the cottage.

Burns was, of course, a great lover, but other habits have been exaggerated and disputed. He published his first poems in Kilmarnock in 1786 as he was wanting to flee the country under threat of prosecution from his girlfriend's father (the father of Jean Armour whom he later married). He died in another house in Dumfries in 1796, aged only 37 having suffered ill health all his life.

Burns is to the Scots as Churchill was to the English during the Second World War – completely idolised as their Master, Lord and King. There is not a word that adequately describes the reverence in which he is held. It is not for English folk to describe his works (even though they may have lived for some years in Scotland) and nor will we attempt to do so.

The cottage was an Ale House between about 1800 and 1881 when it was purchased by the Trustees. Its preservation has been undertaken by people with inspiration, and the result is both awe-inspiring yet quaint. It is certainly one of those cottages that you must visit (and, of course, if you are Scottish it must be top of your list). It has recently been rethatched after a fire.

Goss version

Arcadian

Willow and Thistle (the same)

Leadbeater

Two similar models of this cottage were produced by Willow – the nicer is 10.5cm long, 6.0cm deep and 7.2cm high, while the second has the Thistle China trademark and is 10.8cm long, 6.6cm deep (maximum) and 7.2cm high. The same or similar mould could have been used to produce the larger of two very attractive models by Arcadian, the larger is 10.5cm long, 6.0cm deep (max) and 7.3cm high and the smaller model 6.9cm long and 3.8cm deep and 4.1cm high. A model of unique size by Leadbeater is 7.0cm long, 4.0cm deep and 5.1cm high with an inscription on the side. Smaller Willow Art models are 6.8cm long, 3.7cm deep and 4.0cm high, with the most interesting one being 9.5cm long, 5.3cm deep and 6.7cm high. The small Arcadian model mould was later used to produce models for the 1938 Empire Exhibition in Glasgow (see No. 14 – Glasgow, An Clachan). Those by Goss are also in two sizes and are found either glazed or unglazed. The night-light is 14.9cm long, 8.1cm deep and 8.6 cm high, while the small model is 6.2cm long, 3.5cm deep and 3.7cm high.

Llywelyn Cottage, Beddgelert. 2813.

BEDDGELERT, NORTH WALES

3 Prince Llewelyn's House

Some 700 years ago, according to a sad legend, Prince Llewelyn went hunting leaving his infant son with his dog Gelert to guard him. When the prince returned he found the cradle overturned and blood everywhere. Thinking that Gelert had killed his son, Prince Llewelyn slew the dog only to discover that the baby was safe and Gelert had killed a wolf threatening the child's life.

At the time this event was said to have occurred, Llewelyn's Cottage was a small hunting lodge made of local stone and old ships' timbers, some of which remain today. Although it was extended in the 18th century when stairs were built and the slate roof was raised by some five feet it is still small, and remains typical of the area. Today it serves as the National Trust centre.

The village of Beddgelert in north west Wales where the cottage stands is situated in a beautiful valley and is overlooked by Mount Snowdon. Gelert's grave is a short walk away.

The cottage, not one of W H Goss's best creations, is pleasing in its glazed form but rather indifferent in its unglazed form. It measures 6.4cm long, 3.3cm deep and 5.2cm high.

BUNYAN'S
COTTAGE,
ELSTOW,
BEDFORD.

BEDFORD, BEDFORDSHIRE

4 Bunyan's Cottage, Elstow

Unfortunately, none of the places in and around Bedford where John Bunyan, the author of *Pilgrim's Progress*, was born in 1628, still stand. But there are at least models by Goss and Willow of the cottage at Elstow where he set up house with his first very young wife in the mid-seventeenth century.

A Nonconformist lay preacher, he was twice imprisoned under the Stuart restoration for his outspoken beliefs. It was while serving a final six months sentence that he completed his powerful religious narrative, *Pilgrim's Progress* (1678). An allegory which traces the life of the man Christian from his conversion to his death, it has been published in 200 languages and is almost as widely read in some quarters as the Bible.

His blind daughter Mary, was born in the Elstow cottage, which was originally thatched, but given a tiled roof in the eighteenth century. It was pulled down in 1968 to make way for road improvements, a pity, because it had itself been a place of pilgrimage. Bunyan's second wife, Elizabeth, bore him further children, but he died in London at the age of 60 in 1688, ironically only a year before Nonconformist meeting houses were given legal status.

Coloured models of this important cottage are extremely rare. The Goss model measures 6cm wide, 3.1cm deep and 5.4cm high. The second model is clearly marked 'Willow Art China Longton' and is 7.8cm wide, 5.4cm deep at the gutter and 8cm high. It is not named although it is certainly Bunyan's Cottage. Although rare, the effect is more pedestrian than the Goss version, highlighting the genius of W H Goss in comparison to other makers.

Goss

Willow

Harvard at the time of the American Revolution. Holden Chapel at left, Massachusetts Hall at right. Picture by Pierre du Simitiere, 1767.

BOSTON, USA

5 Holden Chapel and
6 Massachusetts Hall

Both of Harvard University, Cambridge, near Boston, USA

We were very fortunate on visiting these buildings to have such good weather, the sun and snow together allowing Maggie to take some excellent photographs.

In 1638, only 21 years after the Pilgrim Fathers landed at Plymouth, Massachusetts, New England, taxes were being levied, a board of overseers had been appointed and the first students were attending Harvard, the oldest institution of higher learning in the New World. In this same year, the principal instigator in its founding, John Harvard – London-born, and

Cambridge educated – had died at the age of 30.

None of the earliest college buildings still stand. The oldest in existence, Massachusetts Hall built in 1720, is a graceful, well-proportioned structure typical of the American Colonial architectural style. Set amongst mature trees and lawns, it has always provided accommodation for students. The statue on the face of the model is that of James Russell Lowell, Professor of French and Spanish Languages and Literature and Professor of Belles-Lettres 1855-1886. The statue has been removed from the actual building since the model was made.

Second in age is Holden Chapel which dates from 1744. It is considered by many to be the most perfect example of a Georgian building to be seen in America 'a solitary English daisy in a field of Yankee dandelions.' Handsomely blazoned over the doors at each end are the coat of arms

Holden Chapel

of the Holden family, the widow and daughters of Samuel Holden, a prominent English dissenter and Governor of the Bank of England, having been its chief benefactors.

Constructed as a chapel, it had, by the end of the century, become the home of the newly founded medical school, and was used for demonstrations of human dissection. During the War of Independence, it housed Revolutionary troops fighting the British. Today, it is the home of the Harvard Glee Club.

Only night-light models were made of the two American buildings, both being extremely rare. Although Goss is known to have produced a coloured version of Massachusetts Hall none has as yet been found - there are two known white glazed models in existence which were produced for Jones, McDuffee & Stratton of 33,

Franklin St, Boston, Mass. Both are the same size 17.2cm wide, 7.8cm deep and 10.2cm high.

Holden Chapel, also by Goss measures 13.9cm wide, 9.9cm deep and 10.8cm high overall. The model lacks the brilliant blue which backs the Holden arms in real life.

An extra note to collectors: There is a link between Harvard and Stratford-on-Avon. The nineteenth-century novelist Marie Corelli bought and restored Harvard House, a Tudor cottage in Stratford, where John Harvard's mother and grandparents lived. She did this at the behest of a wealthy Chicagoan, Edward Morris, who presented the house to Harvard University in 1909.

A remarkable three-storey model of this cottage exists and is known to be by Willow. (See No. 92)

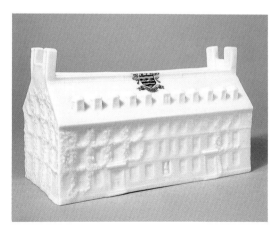

Massachusetts Hall

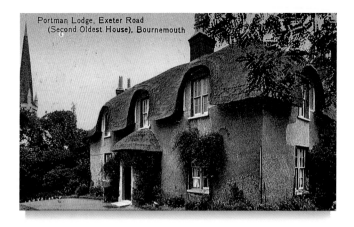

Portman Lodge, Exeter Road
(Second Oldest House), Bournemouth

BOURNEMOUTH, HANTS

7 Portman Lodge

This house, dating from about 1812, was the second to be built in Bournemouth. A four-roomed thatched cottage (later extended), it was put up by Louis Tregonwell, a captain of the Dorset Yeomanry, for his butler, Symes. The first house was Tregonwell Mansion, which had originally been tenanted by a Lady Exeter.

Captain Tregonwell was responsible for coastal defences during the incessant wars with Napoleon's France. He also assisted with the control of smugglers.

The cottage, which stood at the junction of Exeter Road and Exeter Park Road, became known as Portman Lodge after Captain Tregonwell's death, when his widow went to live in it and gave it her own maiden name.

It was damaged by fire in June 1922 and restored only to be demolished in 1930 to make way for the Hants and Dorset Bus Company. When it was torn down, an underground chamber was found three feet below ground level, giving rise to the belief that Symes may have been in league with the very smugglers his master was trying to subdue.

The model by Goss is shaped like a reverse capital 'L', being 6.9cm across the front, 8.2cm deep (excluding the lovely thatch overhang) and 4.4cm high. A rare closed door variation exists.

BUXTON, DERBYSHIRE

8 The Cat and Fiddle Inn

This busy public house and eating place is over 500 years old. It was popular at the turn of the century because at 1,690 feet above sea level it was and is believed to be the highest licensed pub in England. It lies on the A64 Buxton to Macclesfield road in the middle of bleak moorland and at the turn of the century could only be reached with some difficulty whatever the mode of transport. Old postcards link all kinds of transport with the pub, which featured in many famous events, such as The Tour of Britain Milk Cycle Race, whilst one Macclesfield gent walked to Buxton and back, all 22 miles – backwards. In winter however, it is a different story when the road is often closed by heavy snow drifts.

The name 'The Cat and Fiddle' is said to be derived from 'Caton la Fidele' – Caton the faithful who was Governor of Calais and held the city against the French with his followers. Their war cry became 'Caton la Fidele'. One of his followers built the original house and named it after the Governor.

Postcards allow us to follow the buildings' progress in terms of extensions: the original building was as the Goss example, with its little porch on the front and a single story outhouse with a tall chimney on the left. Some time after the First World War the outhouse was demolished to make way for a two storey extension equal in size to 'The Cat and Fiddle' and subsequently a single-storey building was added to the right – now a bar with extensions to the rear. Finally, the porch has been rebuilt with a shaped roof rather than the original flat roof, incorporating the 'The Cat and Fiddle' plaque which was originally above it.

A very attractive and solid looking model was made by Goss, 6.7cm wide, 7.0 cm deep and 6.1cm high, and an unmarked model, or a model sometimes marked Kensington China measures 9.7cm wide, 6.6cm deep and 9.3cm high.

Goss

Kensington China

21

CHRISTCHURCH, HAMPSHIRE

9 The Old Court House

Deeds relating to this house date back to 1236 when the annual rent was a pair of gloves worth a penny. The building is timber-framed and the original wattle and daub was replaced by Tudor bricks. The structure itself must have undergone changes at the same time, as a strong Tudor influence is obvious.

The original court house, which linked up with the Priory Church, was next door and was pulled down either in the late eighteenth or early nineteenth century. The present building was known as the Old Leet House, so-called from the early 1800s when the court leet, which dealt with petty offences, manor affairs and local matters, including appointing officers to act as bread-weighers and ale-tasters, inspectors of chimneys and mantles, and management of the fishing rights at Mudeford Run. The court was discontinued in 1920, and the upper rooms in which it sat are now empty.

The lower part of the building was generally a shop. Photographs from around 1860 show it as a boot and shoe shop. Then, when the owner, Mr Head, emigrated to New Zealand, it became a pork butcher's shop with an open front. The windows were replaced when it was transformed into a book shop, before changing to a perfumery shop in 1939. It is tastefully arranged within and the outside has recently been repainted and a new thatched ridge added. The old court house is owned by the local council.

The attractive, L-shaped Goss model must be handled carefully as the chimneys are very vulnerable. It measures 7.6cm wide, 6.2cm deep and 7.1cm high.

CUMBRIA

10 Cockermouth &
17 Dove Cottage, Grasmere

Homes of William Wordsworth.

William Wordsworth's family came to
Cockermouth from Yorkshire. His father, John,
was a land agent for Sir James Lewther who
owned the house on the main street of
Cockermouth where William was born on 7
April 1770. The River Derwent flowing at the
foot of the garden undoubtedly nurtured the
boy's love of nature which was to be expressed
so intensely in his poetry.

The house, a north-country version of a mid-
Georgian house built in 1745 for the sheriff of
Cumberland, Joshua Lucock, is still much as it
was in Wordsworth's day, with its rubble walling,

windows set in stone architraves and front
porch. It has recently been painted a pink
sandstone colour believed to have been the
original colour. The window frames are grey and
white and the pillars are grey.

Wordsworth and his sister Dorothy rented
Dove Cottage at Grasmere in the Lake District
in 1799 at a cost of £5.00 a year plus six shillings
window tax. Three years later he brought his
bride, Mary Hutchinson, to the cottage and it
remained his home during his most productive
years. It also became a magnet for a large circle
of other poets, writers, painters, philosophers
and scientists. The poem 'Michael' was published
whilst William lived there.

The cottage, originally an inn called 'The Dove
and Olive Bough', is a lovely two-storey building
which may date from early in the eighteenth

Cockermout

Dove Cottage

century. It has three rooms downstairs, a cold room cooled by spring water and four bedrooms upstairs, one of which Wordsworth added to accommodate his growing family. Even so, it proved too small and in 1813, he let it to Thomas de Quincey, and moved to Rydal Mount a few miles south of Grasmere. He was living there when he was appointed Poet Laureate in 1843 and died there in 1850.

Wordsworth's birthplace at Cockermouth is owned by the National Trust and Dove Cottage by the Trustees of Dove Cottage. The museum adjacent to the latter contains splendid exhibits of the poet's life and times.

Goss models of both cottages are unglazed. The model of his birthplace measures 8.2cm wide, 4.9cm deep (maximum) and 5.6cm high. Dove Cottage is 10.3cm wide overall, 8.5cm deep and 5.9cm high.

Dove Cottage was also made by Carlton. Our favourite non-Goss cottage, it measures 8.7cm wide, 7.5cm deep and 4.9cm high.

Dove Cottage by Carlton

Dove Cottage by Goss

CRICCIETH, GWYNDD, WALES

11 Early home of David Lloyd George

Although David Lloyd George was born in Manchester in 1863, where his father William was a school teacher and a Baptist, he spent most of his youth in Llanystumdwy, his mother's native village. She had returned to her childhood home with David and his brother following her husband's death. They lived with her brother, Richard Lloyd, who had succeeded his father as the local shoemaker.

William George, Lloyd's father, had been much influenced by Robert Owen, the Welsh pioneer in co-operative socialism, and young David's thinking had been moulded in this direction. His leanings were intensified by the poverty he saw in Llanystumdwy and he developed a passionate interest in politics. He did very well at the local Anglican school although he rebelled against its church teaching.

He qualified as an attorney in 1884 and used the courts to gain renown as a radical Liberal. In 1888 he founded his first newspaper, *The Trumpet of Freedom* at Pwllheli and eventually in 1890 he was elected to Parliament where he instituted far-reaching social reforms. He became Prime Minister in 1916 and lead a strong cabinet during World War 1, waging war aggressively, but playing a moderating role in shaping the Treaty of Versailles. Ousted from office in 1922, he nevertheless continued to be politically active until his death in 1945.

The cottage at Llanystumdwy, an attractive building which has changed little since Lloyd George lived there, is made of large chunks of local stone and roofed with slate, and opens directly onto the street. It has recently been refurbished and furnished with period cottage furniture, while the shoemaker's shop has been fitted out appropriately and is now a museum open to the public. The Prime Minister's burial place and the Lloyd George Museum are both within walking distance.

Goss made two versions of the cottage, the majority depicting not only the living quarters but also an annexe with a separate entrance, which was his uncle's cobbler's shop. This version measures 10.2cm wide, 4.0cm deep and 5.4cm high. The rare version showing the living quarters only is 6.1cm wide, 3.7cm deep and 5.3cm high.

Without cobbler's shop

With cobbler's shop

DORCHESTER, DORSET

12 Thomas Hardy's Birthplace

Thomas Hardy was born in 1840 near Dorchester in a village called Higher Bockhampton. His family were builders and stone masons, and his birthplace, a pleasant thatched house, had been built by his great grandfather in 1800. Thomas started life as an architect, moving to London at 22 to specialise in church restoration. But ill health forced him to return home five years later, when he took up writing.

The woods around the cottage (protected by the Forestry Commission) are the prototype for the heath which featured in his starkly realistic novels about life in the bleak countryside. In particular, *The Return of the Native, Under the Greenwood Tree* and *Far From the Madding Crowd*

were written whilst he lived here between 1872 and 1874. He was married twice, first to Emma Gifford, and after her death, to Florence Dugdale. He moved several times, finally settling in Dorchester in a house called Max Gate, which he designed himself. He died there in 1928 and his ashes were interred in Westminster Abbey.

The house, now owned by the National Trust, is open to the public and is surrounded by a lovely garden. An appointment is necessary to visit the house, although the gardens are open throughout the year. Thomas Hardy's memorabilia are on view at the county museum in Dorchester. Hardy enjoys a loyal American following as a stone near the house testifies.

Goss made the only known model which is difficult to find. It measures 10.4cm long, 3.4cm deep (maximum) and 4.6cm high.

EDINBURGH, SCOTLAND

13 John Knox's House

John Knox, the founder of Scottish Presbyterianism, was born of farming stock at Haddington near Edinburgh in 1505. He was initially a Roman Catholic priest, but, by 1545, had committed himself to the Protestant cause. He was captured by the French around 1550 when St Andrew's Castle was taken. After rowing in galleys for 19 months, the English government secured his release in 1552. He was briefly a royal chaplain in England and helped prepare the second *Book of Common Prayer*. When the Catholic Mary 'Bloody Mary' came to the throne, he fled into exile and spent some time in Geneva with the French Protestant reformer John Calvin. In 1559, he returned to Scotland to lead the fight against Roman Catholicism there and was installed as first Minister of Edinburgh, a post he held until his death in 1572.

The house in which he lived from 1563 stands about half-way along the Royal Mile on the north side, projecting out into the street. It belonged to a James Mosman and his wife, Mariota Arres, who had had to carry out extensive rebuilding, after it had been burned down by the English in 1544. During the reconstruction, the Mosmans set their ceremonial bearings with their initials, IM and MA, on the west wall.

The building fell into decay and was seriously damaged when the neighbouring house collapsed in 1839-40. In 1846 the Free Church bought it, intending to demolish it to widen the street, but when this became known there was a public outcry, and, after incomplete repairs, it became a Knox museum. In 1900 it passed to the United Free Church, and in 1929 became the property of the Church of Scotland. During extensive repairs in 1958, many ancient features were discovered. The Netherbow Theatre, now a part of the John Knox complex was added in 1990 and marks the original site of the main gate to Edinburgh.

Cottages were produced both by Goss England and Willow Art, possibly using the same mould. Both are unglazed. The Goss models have black chimney pots and doors; those by Willow are brown. They are both 6.8cm wide, 5.0cm deep and 10.1cm high.

GLASGOW, 1938 EMPIRE EXHIBITION

14 An Clachan

The great Empire Exhibition of 1938 featured within its boundaries a large area known as the Clachan. This consisted of a collection of authentically reproduced 'Highland and Island' buildings sited amongst mature trees, with rolling grassland, a loch and a burn, and linked by trodden by-ways.

Clachan is the gaelic word for a Highland village, and an *an clachan* is a single cottage within that village. In this show village, the architect, Dr Colin Sinclair, brought together different types of crofting cottages from various parts of Scotland. Two Hebridean black-houses with six-foot thick sloping walls and rounded gables, demonstrated the crofters' expertise, acquired over 1,000 years, in combatting the harsh Atlantic winter weather.

The Skye cottage had a thatch of moor grass held in place by ropes weighted at each end with stones. The Argyll cottage had a proper standing chimney, indicating that the weather there was not so harsh as elsewhere.

The village was demolished in about 1940 as a wartime measure, because it was close to shipping lanes and might have served as a landmark. We have been unable to ascertain which of the cottages were the so-called prototypes for these models but it seemed likely that the 'Argyll' *an clachan* inspired one of them. In fact, Goss England simply revamped existing moulds by recolouring them and marking them with the Red Lion and 'An Clachan'.

The Arcadian 'Jean MacAlpine's Inn' An Clachan was modelled on a cottage at Aberfoyle (No. 44) and is 10.3 cm long, 5.4 cm deep and 5.5 cm high, whilst the Goss 'Burns' An Clachan is 6.4 cm long, 3.5 cm deep and 3.7 cm high. This was probably the Arcadian 'Burns' mould (No. 2).

Goss England models from Arcadian moulds

Empire Exhibition lion

15 The Abbot's Kitchen &
16 The Church of Joseph of Arimathoea

The fourteenth-century **Abbot's Kitchen** was the only part of the ancient monastery at Glastonbury to survive the devastation wrought during the dissolution in 1539. It had been built to cater for the Abbot's guests rather than the monks, who led a frugal existence. The building is basically square with the corners lopped off to form fireplaces; it is crowned by a chimney.

The Church of Joseph of Arimathoea, if it existed, is thought to have been the first Christian place of worship in Britain. It was built around AD 60 by followers of Joseph of Arimathoea. Legend has it that he was a rich Jerusalem merchant who may have been an uncle of Jesus as well as a disciple. He is said to have removed Christ's body from the cross and deposited it in his own tomb. Some time after the death of Jesus, followers of the new religion were forced to flee. Joseph, allegedly with the Holy Grail, sailed via Brittany and Wales to Glastonbury, where he founded the abbey.

A church on the site was destroyed by fire in 1184. There are no records of its appearance and Goss created his model from a hypothetical drawing at the British Museum. It probably had timber pillars and framework: was wattled inside and out, and thatched with reeds.

The 1184 fire destroyed not only the church but all of the other Abbey buildings. They were reconstructed, only to be destroyed again at the dissolution. The site was eventually bought for the Church of England through public subscription. King Arthur was reputedly born a few miles from Glastonbury and buried in about AD516 nearby in the mythical Isle of Avalon.

The only known models of both church and kitchen are by Goss. They are unglazed and extremely rare. There are two versions of the kitchen, one with a red door, the second with a black. Both are 6.9cm square and 8.9cm high. The church is 7cm wide, 3.6cm deep and 3.9cm high.

Above: The Abbot's Kitchen. Left: The Church of Joseph of Arimathoa

29

17 Wordsworth's Dove Cottage, Grasmere,

is combined with No. 10, his birthplace at Cockermouth

GRETNA GREEN, SCOTLAND

18 The Old Toll Bar, and
72 Old Blacksmith's Shop and Marriage Room

Between 1753 and 1856, Gretna Green was the centre of the runaway marriage traffic 'industry' because it was the first settlement inside Scotland where if a single man and woman could declare themselves husband and wife in the presence of two witnesses they were in fact legally married. In 1753, irregular marriages had been made illegal in England, including 'Fleet weddings' conducted near Fleet Prison, London, and the industry and the 'parson' moved to Gretna Green. Here he presided over marriages of eloping couples often between a young girl of wealthy parents who had fallen in love with a young man considered wholly unsuitable perhaps due to his lowly position in life (for example, a footman). In 1856, however, in response to such practices, a new Marriage Act meant that one of the couple to be married had to be resident in Scotland for 21 days and the runaway traffic declined. Ironically, the man most influential in changing the law had himself been married at Gretna Green. Nevertheless, weddings at Gretna Green did not cease completely and couples would go into hiding for the required period.

The romantic image persists today and many people get 'married again' over the anvil, although in the last century it was a much more serious matter.

The **Old Toll Bar** (18) was built about 1830, being erected for the sole purpose of collecting tolls from the England to Scotland traffic. The semi-circular room to the front and centre was the room in which over 10,000 marriage ceremonies were conducted.

Perhaps the rarest of all the British Goss models, it measures 12.7cm wide, 10.1cm deep and 6.7cm high. A model by Grafton is 12.6cm long, 6.3cm deep and 4.2cm high.

Grafton

Goss

The Blacksmith's Shop and Marriage Room (72) is on the old coaching road from Carlisle – the A6071 – and marriages 'over the anvil' were popular until 1830 when a new road, the A74, replaced the A6071 as the main road into Scotland and the Toll Bar on the Scottish side of the Sark Bridge became the first choice of eloping couples.

The Blacksmith's Shop was built around 1712 and is the most notorious of the marriage rooms, having been visited by many famous persons, including their Majesties King George V and Queen Mary, in 1916. The building houses a collection of coaches which is a reminder of the history of romantic Gretna Green.

The cottages were produced by Willow Art and Arcadian and measure 8.5cm wide, 6.1cm deep and 5.5cm high, whilst a larger and rarer model, unmarked, measures 10.8cm wide, 6.6cm deep (overall) and 6.8cm high. A further very rare model by Willow, produced before 1910, measures 6cm wide, 3.5cm deep and 3.7cm high.

Unmarked

Arcadian and Willow

Rare early Willow version

GULLANE, EAST LOTHIAN
SCOTLAND

19 Gullane Smithy

Gullane, or Golyn as it was known in medieval times, has been inhabited for thousands of years, as ancient remains and the much later twelfth-century church testify. The old smithy, which dates from the seventeenth century, was built at a time when Gullane was beginning to be choked to death by encroaching sand. It was eventually abandoned and a new village called Dirleton was created a mile to the east.

The smithy, built of rubble and pantiles, is now owned by the East Lothian District Council who restored it after it had become derelict in the 1930s. The building has always been a popular subject for artists. Postcards were produced early in this century when 'Sandy' Darg, a blacksmith, occupied it until his death in 1915. His predecessors had been connected with Gullane since the 18th century. Today his old blacksmith's tools are in the care of the council. The smithy has since served as a petrol station, a shop selling games equipment and an arts and craft centre. It is now a gift and card shop.

The Goss model, coloured red and fawn, includes the old brick extension to the chimney, often damaged and always off the vertical. It is 7.4cm long, 4.9cm wide and 5.2cm high.

HEADCORN, KENT

20 Hop Kiln

Headcorn is in the middle of Kent, the garden of England – the centre of England's hop and fruit growing county; an industry that was perhaps more important up to the beginning of this century than now but is still significant today and popular with tourists.

"Curious towers with conical tops,

They're hundreds strong in the land of hops."

(From *The Enchanted Road* by the Kent poet Donald Maxwell)

In 1956 a survey of Kent oasts conducted by the Kent Council of Social Services looking into the preservation of Rural Kent studied 650 oasts as a result of which 42 became listed buildings. This was not one of them, possibly because although modelled by Goss, this Hop Kiln, is an annex to the 'stowage', whilst other hop kilns are an integral part of the barn or stowage building. This kiln, on the south side of town, is one of two in Headcorn which were still standing early this century – the other being knocked down about 1920. The conical shaped 50 foot high Hop Kiln was built in the early 1800s when small round kilns were first erected, roundels proving cheaper to build and more efficient than the previous square buildings in whose corners the

Goss

Carlton

33

A working kiln

The hop kiln today

hops failed to dry. Here, hops for drying were placed high in the kiln about 20cms deep on a grid of latticed wood covered by a wire or horse hair mat. Heat from the anthracite furnace, with sulphur for fumigating and colouring, rose up through the hops and out of the cowl which pulled the moisture and fumes out of the kiln.

Hop drying was a very skilled process and the hop dryer, who regulated the kiln temperature to prevent scorching or discolouration, was considered the most important man on the hop farm. Fresh hops are 75% to 83% moisture and the moisture content has to be reduced to about 6%. Thus to produce one ton of dried hops, three tons of water has to be driven off in a continuous process lasting for several days. After drying, the hops are placed in golden heaps to cool in the 'stowage' area and then pressed in cylindrical sacks or 'pockets', two metres long, before being transported to the brewery.

The Headcorn Kiln fell into disrepair as a result of a bomb during the 1939/45 war. In 1969 it was bought by Mr and Mrs Woodruff who saved it from demolition and undertook extensive repair works using similarly old timbers and obtaining a 'cowl' from another identical building at Hastings.

Although we cannot guarantee this was the 'Headcorn' hop kiln copied by Goss, its general shape and such details as the final circle of angled bricks (the dentil or dog's tooth layer) immediately before the roof are convincing. The size is 3.6cm diameter x 9.3cm high.

An interesting but unnamed model of a hop kiln by Carlton is well made and nicely coloured red and brown. Its proportions (5cm diameter x 9.7cm high) show it was not modelled on the Headcorn Hop Kiln and perhaps one of our readers can suggest a provenance.

ILFRACOMBE, DEVON

21 Old Maids' Cottage Lee

This attractive thatched cottage is said by some to have been built in the seventeenth century, while others date it only to 1763. It is quite large with four bedrooms, and the slate for the floors was probably quarried locally.

It was part of the vast Drake-Cutcliffe estate which was broken up when it fell into the bailiff's hands in 1900. Three old maids lived in it at the time, and it had no electricity or running water. It is often called the Three Old Maids' Cottage, perhaps as a result of the anonymous poem *A Bird in Hand*. In this poem what start as three 'young maids of Lee' turn into old maids by the end due to their fastidiousness in choosing a partner:

> "There are three old maids at Lee,
> They are cross as cross can be,
> And there they are, and there they'll be,
> To the end of the chapter, one two, three,
> These three old maids of Lee!"

A further confusion is that the Three Old Maids of Lee have also been depicted as three shire horses but there can be no connection with the cottage which had no stables. It has, unfortunately, been closed to the public since it was taken over by a new owner in the 1950s.

THE OLD MAIDS COTTAGE, LEE. Nr ILFRACOMBE

The pretty Goss model is partly thatched and exists both glazed and unglazed. It is 7.3cm long, 4.1cm deep (maximum overall) and 4.4cm high. Willow also produced two attractive models – one with a brown roof, the other with a yellow, which, like a third, by Grafton, are not to proper scale. The Willow models are 5.9cm long, 3.6cm deep and 4.5cm high. The Grafton is 6.7cm long, 4.7cm deep and 6.6cm high.

Above: Grafton. Above right: Goss.
Right: Willow

ILFRACOMBE, DEVON

22 St Nicholas Chapel

St Nicholas Chapel, also known as the Ancient Chapel or the Old Chapel, stands on Lantern Hill which was probably an island at high tide before the sea receded.

The chapel was built around 1320 although the first documented reference occurred in 1416. It has been used for many purposes over the years, firstly as a chapel for the families who lived around the harbour – St Nicholas being the patron saint of sailors. St Nicholas is also the patron saint of scholars and during the chapel's early years the priest would teach the local boys in the upper room of the chapel.

The Bishop of Exeter recorded in 1522 that "In the chapel of St Nicholas erected above the harbour of the town of Ilfracombe a certain light is found burning on the summit year by year – like a twinkling star by night." It is also claimed that in 1795 the women of the village climbed the hills and walked the walls of the chapel with their red petticoats thrown over their shoulders in order to make the French believe that soldiers were on guard.

From 1835 to 1871 it was converted into a home and occupied by John Davie, his wife and their 14 children. More recently it has served as a reading room, a laundry and even as a place for band practice. It is now owned by Ilfracombe UDC.

Built from stone excavated from the hill on which it stands, the chapel appears to grow out of the living rock. It was after its secularisation that the large lantern was built on the west end of the roof in 1650. Much of the original woodwork from ships' timbers is still extant.

In recent years restoration work has been carried out on the oriel window in the north wall, which was where the priest kept the light of St Nicholas burning.

Glazed and unglazed models, and a pale variation of this cottage with a white roof, by Goss measure 7.2cm long, 4.9cm deep and 5.5cm high.

The glazed cottage produced by Grafton (7.2cm long, 5.2cm deep and 6.3cm high) and the unglazed version by Willow Art (6.7cm long, 4.3cm deep and 5.6cm high) both make a basic error in showing the lantern with red windows all round, whilst in reality the chapel only has red windows towards the sea.

Willow

Grafton

Goss

ISLE OF MAN

23 Manx Cottage

This cottage in its original form no longer exists, but was probably Old Pete's Cottage situated at Ballure half a mile south of Ramsey and four miles north of Laxey, Isle of Man. Old Pete's real name was John Kinnish and he was immortalised as Old Pete with his cottage in a novel by Hall Cain, *The Manx Man*, published in 1887. (Apparently, neither man liked the other, Old Pete, a real character and very down to earth, would pour over the Bible, having taught himself to read when he was middle-aged, whilst Hall Cain was upper middle class and well-educated).

In Old Pete's time the coach from Douglas, through Laxey, to Ramsey would stop outside Pete's and tourists could look round his house festooned with knick-knacks, purchased in bulk,

then suitably positioned and soiled. These Old Pete could then be 'persuaded' to part with at a price reflecting the sorrow that the loss of such a personal item would cause. 'Old Pete' died in September 1906 aged 66 and many hundreds attended his funeral. Left unoccupied and the roof gone, the clay, straw and mortar walls crumbled, leaving only the foundations visible today.

Manx thatch is completely different from mainland thatch in that it is laid on turf, the grass uppermost and the roots often forming the ceiling of the house, supported by lathes on rafters or planks and sometimes whitewashed. The most common thatching material is wheat straw, but heather (ling), Marram grass (Agrostis) or reeds are used and all, when laid, have to be held in by herring net and ropes tied to projecting stones built into the external walls. The material used for Old Pete's cottage was probably reed on plank - as witness old postcards. The thatch only lasts three years and nowadays the money and the availability of suitable craftsmen required to maintain the tradition are hard to find. They may, however, be seen at Craigneash, Isle of Man.

There are two Goss models, a night-light measuring 12.7cm long, 8.1cm deep and 9.3cm high, and a small model at 6.2cm long, 4.3cm deep overall and 4.7cm high.

Another maker, possibly Willow, also modelled the cottage. This version known as 'Pete's Cottage' measures 5.6cm long, 3.4cm deep and 3.9cm high.

Goss small version

Goss night-light

Pete's Cottage

KIRRIEMUIR, TAYSIDE, SCOTLAND

24 A Window in Thrums

This is the title of one of the lesser-known works of Sir James Matthew Barrie, who is best remembered for *Peter Pan*, *The Admirable Crichton*, *Quality Street* and *What Every Woman Knows*. The cottage of the same name, is the place from which Barrie supposedly viewed 'Thrums' as he rechristened Kirriemuir. The name Thrums had an added significance being a type of thread used by local weavers, a profession to which his father belonged. Barrie actually lived opposite while writing both this and *The Little Minister*.

The cottage is at the top of a brae which would have afforded a fine view of the town before the advertising hoardings which stand there now were erected. Barrie was born in nearby Brechin Road in May 1860, in a house which today houses the Barrie museum and the original Wendy House (the old wash house).

'A Window in Thrums' is the northernmost of the cottages modelled. There are two Goss models both glazed and unglazed. The night-light is one of the rarest of its genre and measures 12.9cm long x 7.8cm deep and 11cm high. The smaller plain form is 6cm wide x 3.5cm deep and 5.1cm high. A third rendering of the cottage by Carlton is different from those by Goss, having the typical Carlton grey roof and measuring 5.7cm wide, 3.8cm deep and 5.6cm high.

Goss

Carlton

Goss night-light

Goss night-light

Willow

LAND'S END, CORNWALL

25 First and Last House

Land's End, forming the most westerly point of the British mainland, is one of the most famous of all English landmarks. With the exception of the Lizard, it is also the furthest south, pointing a finger into the Atlantic Ocean towards America.

The so-called 'first and last house' on the point (depending on whether you're coming or going), may date from the end of the seventeenth century, and stands on the site of a shepherd's hut believed to have been built in the 1600s. The present building is of local stone with a slate roof and is painted blue and white.

In the 1860s, it was owned by Grace Thomas, who used to walk from Sennen some four miles along the coastal path every day to sell cake, bread, ginger beer, lemonade and souvenirs to visitors. In 1905, her son William relinquished the tenancy to Edith James, who commissioned the Goss cottages. Her son, H T James, ordered the second of two Arcadian cottages, produced after 1931 and marked "First and Last Refreshment House in England, H T James."

Land's End attracts nearly a million visitors a year, and its present owner is The Lands End and John O' Groats Company Ltd who have installed a craft shop in the cottage.

The house was enlarged in the 1920s, before which time Goss had produced two models – a

Goss small

FIRST AND LAST HOUSE, LANDS END

night-light measuring 12.4cm wide, 10.4cm deep and 11.4cm high and a small plain model 6.7cm wide, 5.2cm deep and 6.2cm high. The latter may have grey, cream or brown roofs; both come glazed and unglazed. Willow made an 8.5cm, white model with a green door and a crest. A very rare, glazed Arcadian model, without annex, but with the Land's End crest, is 6.7cm wide, 5.6cm deep and 6.8cm high. After the annex was added Goss made one of their rarest and longest cottages at 14.2cm long, 4.9cm deep and 6cm high. An almost identical Arcadian cottage is 13.8cm long, 4.6cm deep and 6.1cm high. This does not bear the H T James caption, which only appears on the post-1931 Arcadian version – 9.8cm long, 5.2cm deep and 5.7cm high.

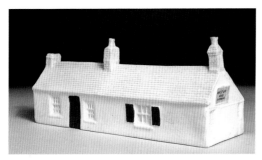

Goss with annex

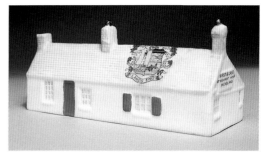

Arcadian

Arcadian without annex

Arcadian

LEDBURY, HEREFORDSHIRE

26 Feathers Hotel and
27 Old Market House

The Feathers Hotel and the Old Market House can be seen near each other in this lovely old county town.

Feathers Hotel
This sixteenth-century hotel was a coaching inn when Ledbury was a stopping place for the Royal Mail en route between Cheltenham and Aberystwyth. The coaching yard was behind the main building and above it, supported by pillars, were the assembly rooms. The building has masses of beams both inside and out, and until the end of the last century, its outer walls were covered with plaster. It is said to have been a favourite honeymoon hotel early in this century,

when honeymoon couples were presented with a Goss cottage.

The Old Market House
A beautifully proportioned building thought to date to between 1617 and 1645 by Jack Abell, a builder who worked for Charles I, from money raised by public subscription. It is black and white with brick infill, large windows and a red roof, and its 16 pillars, possibly of Spanish chestnut, have acquired a mellow patina.

Old deeds indicate that rent from the market house was used to provide 12 coats at Christmas for 12 poor persons of Ledbury. At that time it was mainly a store for grain, wool and hops, but was also the site for cock fights and market stalls. More recently, it has been used for meetings, including council meetings. In 1645,

The Market House, Ledbury (No. 1)

the Battle of Ledbury raged around it, when Royalists defeated Cromwell's Roundheads.

The Ledbury cottages produced by Goss are both unglazed. The hotel is 11.5cm long, 4.5cm deep and 6.9cm high; the market house is 6.8cm long, 3.5cm deep and 5.4cm high.

Another unglazed market house, recently discovered, is unmarked, but it is in the solid Leadbeater tradition. It measures 11.5cm long, 6.7cm deep and 10.5cm high.

Goss

Unmarked

LICHFIELD, STAFFORDSHIRE

28 Samuel Johnson's Birthplace

The house where the great man of letters and lexicographer Samuel Johnson was born in 1709 was built by his father the year before, using timbers from a previous building on the same site. Described in 1797 as 'the best house thereabouts', it has changed little in external appearance. It was bought for £250 by the city of Lichfield in 1900 to become a memorial "to the genius and ability of the late Samuel Johnson."

The house had eight rooms, one serving as the shop for Samuel's father and brother who were booksellers, thus surrounding Johnson with books from an early age. The ground floor was later used for various businesses, and, at one time, the Lichfield Mercury had its offices there.

Samuel Johnson, after leaving Oxford, opened a school at Edial Hall near Lichfield where David and Peter Garrick were among his pupils. The venture failed, however, and Johnson and David Garrick together went to London, where the latter found fame as an actor. Johnson meanwhile struggled to make a living, writing articles for newspapers. He also produced essays, poetry, satire, criticism and a play, *Irene*. In 1755 Johnson completed his most famous work, *A Dictionary of the English Language*, noted as much for its highly subjective definitions as for its scholarliness. He received an honorary doctorate from Trinity College, Dublin, in 1765 and died in 1784. He was buried in Westminster Abbey alongside his friend David Garrick.

The Goss model of the house is found both glazed and unglazed, measuring 4.8cm long, 4.2cm deep and 7.6 cm high.

LLANGOLLEN, CLWYD, WALES

29 Plas Newydd

This house, high above Llangollen, was for 50 years the home of "the two most celebrated virgins in Europe", Lady Eleanor Butler and Miss Sarah Ponsonby. The two ladies, both of wealthy Anglo-Irish families, left their homes in 1778 and, while touring Wales looking for a home, they discovered Llangollen which they called "the beautifullest country in the world". They moved into Plas Newydd in May 1780.

The house, dating from at least the beginning of the eighteenth century, was unpretentious until the ladies and subsequent owners began to improve and make additions, such as stained glass oriel windows, carved Gothic oak panels. Noble posts were added to the porch, together with

carved lions given to the ladies by the Duke of Wellington, in a tradition whereby distinguished visitors – among them, Wordsworth, Southey and Wedgwood – were expected to present them with carved oak pieces.

The ladies died in 1829 and 1831. General John Yorke, who bought the house in 1876 added black Elizabethan beams and additional carvings to the exterior. The local district council now own the property, having acquired and opened it to the public in 1933 towards the end of the Goss era.

Goss is said to have made cottages sold locally, but none have come to light. An unmarked model, Reg. No. 521568, probably German, was made in the 1930s, and can still be found. 11.2cm long, 6.7cm deep and 7.7cm high.

The Huer's House, Newquay.

NEWQUAY, CORNWALL

30 Huer's House

Newquay Bay is one of Cornwall's famous surfing resorts. The actual New Quay was built in 1440, when it is probable that the Huer's House, then a Hermitage, already existed. The shape of the windows date it to the fourteenth century. Newquay did not become prosperous until the late eighteenth century when huge shoals of pilchards arrived regularly in the bay. It was probably around this time that the Huer (the man who looked out for the pilchard shoals) took over the cottage on the headland as a shelter from the weather. Certain alterations were made and when it was restored in 1838 by a man named Vivian, payment was in fish.

When the Huer spotted a shoal, he would shout through a horn three feet long, the word 'heva!' Then all hands would turn to. The fish were caught mainly by 'seining companies', usually consisting of three boats, each trailing massive nets more than 400 yards long. Most of the fish were exported to the Continent, chiefly to Spain and Italy.

By the beginning of this century, the pilchards were abandoning the bay and the Huer's House became obsolete. Since then, it has served as a shelter, although, unfortunately, an iron lintel has been used to widen the entrance, thereby changing the house's appearance.

The coloured china model produced only by Goss is oval and comes both glazed and unglazed. It is always grey with black features. 6.6cm long, 5.1cm deep and 5.5cm high.

NEWQUAY, CORNWALL

31 Look-Out House

The original Look-Out House, dating from the Napoleonic wars, was torn down around 1920 when the naval coastguard was disbanded following the end of the First World War. The fame of the site resulting from the campaign in response to this led to the the manufacture of the model. A war memorial was erected on the site and unveiled by the Prince of Wales, Duke of Cornwall (later Edward VIII), in May 1921.

Fortunately we have obtained photographs from before the look-out's demolition showing that it probably had four portholes. The present look-out house, which stands at the end of the same peninsula, was built between the wars and used during World War II.

Some of the Goss china models have four portholes, and others, five. All are glazed and measure 4.8cm in diameter and are 6.6cm high. A larger model by Tuscan, which has only three portholes, is 7.5cm in diameter and 9.2cm high.

Goss

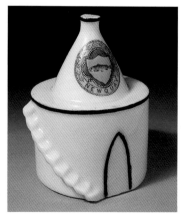

Tuscan

Old thatched cottage, Poole.

POOLE, DORSET

32 The Old Thatched Cottage

This lovely sixteenth-century cottage, the last house in Poole to have had a thatched roof, was demolished in 1919 to make way for 'progress' in the high street in the form of Woolworth's. It was a fine example of Poole's domestic architecture, with walls known as cob, made of gravel and straw. Fortunately, our collection of old postcards has enabled us to determine where the old thatched cottage used to be. Only the cobbles in Carter's Lane to the left of the old cottage and the building to the right, a chemist's shop since 1868, remain much as they were. Where the cottage had stood, a Woolworth's store was built, to be replaced in turn by a Chinese restaurant.

Poole town council are now restoring the best of the old town while at the same time, developing a new shopping centre alongside it, but it's too late for the building on which this, one of our favourite cottages, was modelled. Produced only by Goss, it measures 6.8cm wide, 4cm deep and 5.1cm high, including its vulnerable chimney.

The Priest's House, Prestbury.

PRESTBURY, CHESHIRE

33 Priest's House

Among all the cottages modelled by Goss that we have visited (and we've seen them all), this is one of the prettiest and best maintained. Believed to date from at least the mid-fifteenth century, it has a slate roof, white walls with black beams and decoration, leaded diamond windows with green and rose glass, and an old York stone floor.

Prestbury, situated on the Cheshire-Lancashire border astride the River Bollin, is three miles from Macclesfield and was a monastic settlement when the church was built in the thirteenth century. As the mother church of the parish, it also served 35 local townships. The nave of the church was the place where

local disputes were adjudicated and it also became known as the 'joiners' shop' because so many marriages were performed there.

It is thought that it was from this priest's house that the vicar defied the Roundheads after Cromwell shut down the church in 1448, addressing his parishioners from the first-floor balcony. He also courageously conducted marriage ceremonies here and this practice continued until 1708.

The house is now owned by Westminster Bank, who have preserved it excellently.

A lovely building and a beautiful Goss model: 'L' shaped, 6.8cm across the front, 8.6cm deep and 7.1cm high. The chimney shown at the back of the models disappeared when an extension was added in about 1970.

ROCHESTER, KENT

34 Dickens' House Gads Hill

Charles Dicken's house, Gads Hill, is just off the A26 near Higham village between Gravesend and Rochester. When Dickens was a boy he determined one day to own this fine house, which he had seen during walks with his father, who had said, "If you were to be very persevering and were to work hard, you might some day come to live in it."

He finally bought it in 1855 and wrote *Great Expectations* and *Our Mutual Friend*, among others, here. He died here in June 1870 while working on *The Mystery of Edwin Drood*.

Dickens was born in 1812 in Portsmouth, but the family moved to London, where his father was imprisoned for debt. Poverty-stricken, the boy was forced to leave school and work in a blacking factory, a bitter experience which helped to make him a social reformer. He was a court stenographer and parliamentary reporter before turning to fiction. The most popular author of his time, many of his works were first serialised in newspapers. They were ardent crusades against such abuses as imprisonment for debt, legal delays and inadequate education.

Gad's Hill has been a school for over fifty years, and looks much as it did when Goss (the only potter to do so) produced his cottage. He made two moulds, the earlier of which was inaccurate, neglecting to show the ivy-draped side windows. Both are 6.7cm long, 4.1cm deep and 5.3cm high

ST IVES, CORNWALL

35 St Nicholas' Chapel

The tiny chapel on the island at St Ives overlooks both the sea and the land as does its namesake on the hill at Ilfracombe. Like its namesake, too, the inside is warm, clean, and lovingly cared for.

St Nicholas' chapel is known to have been in existence at least since the end of the fifteenth century when the records show a payment of one shilling and four pence was made for its having been 'mended'. In 1534, there was a light here to guide the ships at sea, while in later years the building was used as a look-out by revenue officers. It may at some time have been a residence, for it had a chimney until the nineteenth century and a fireplace remains.

The war department, which conducted military exercises in the area at the beginning of this century, started to demolish it in 1904, but they got no further than lopping off the chimney before there was a national outcry. The Times carried incensed articles, and a restraining order was enforced.

A local shipowner Sir Edward Hain, had the building restored in 1911 to commemorate the coronation of George V. But it fell into disrepair again, and was restored to its present state in 1971 by J F Holman with the cooperation of the St Ives council. It was used as a set for a film about the sinking of the Titanic and when a gale ripped off part of the roof during shooting, it was replaced by the film company. The building is now maintained by nearby churches and is open to the public. Goss probably produced his model at the time of the national battle to save the chapel, but despite that it lacks inspiration. Both glazed and unglazed models measure 5.5cm long, 3.5cm deep and 4.9cm to the top of the cross.

Post Office, Sennen, Land's End.

SENNEN, CORNWALL

36 First & Last Post Office near Lands End

The original post office, a thatched building dating from the seventeenth century, has been altered to such an extent that it is hardly recognisable. Formerly with two storeys comprising a shop and residence to the left and a single storey post office to the right, it was made into two full storeys in about 1930, when the thatch was replaced by slate. It has now been extended to house a small supermarket, and the post office has been transferred to a shop on the opposite side of the road. Not in itself worth a visit, but you will pass it on your way to the 'First and Last House'.

Goss, the only one to model this cottage, reproduced it in its 1913 form complete with thatch. Glazed and unglazed versions are 7.3cm wide, 3.5cm deep (maximum) and 4.4cm high.

SHALLOWFORD, STAFFORDSHIRE

37 Izaak Walton's birthplace

Izaak Walton is famous for his book *The Compleat Angler* first published in 1653. He was born at a different location on 9 August 1593 into a poor family and was probably self educated. He became a Freeman of the Ironmongers Company, an honorary title, possibly as a result of his biographies, for Ironmongery was not his trade. His first wife died in 1640, their seven children having already died in their infancy and childhood. His second wife was Ann Ken, whose half brother was Bishop Thomas Ken, the hymn writer. Izaak had a son and daughter, became wealthy and was able on his death in 1683 to bequeath London houses and farmsteads to Stafford town for charitable purposes.

This lovely thatched cottage with eyebrow windows was copied by Goss, probably after 1920, when the County Council sold the cottage to the Izaak Walton Trust who opened it as a museum – now part of the Shugborough Museum – in 1924. Unfortunately, sparks from the railway line often set fire to the thatch and in 1939 it was replaced with tiles.

It was never Izaak Walton's permanent home and the museum was meant to show a typical domestic interior of the period. However, apart from old coloured windows, it has been insensitively modernised.

There are three models of this cottage with marginally different features but all are thatched with eyebrow windows. The two Goss models have features on all four sides. Overall measurements for the smaller version are 8.5cm long, 4.1cm deep and 4.8cm high and the larger 9.7cm long, 5.4cm deep and 5.7cm high. The Leadbeater model has no features on the back and measures 13.2cm long, 5.5cm deep and 8cm high. Interestingly, Goss spelt Izaak Walton's name incorrectly as Isaac.

Leadbeater version

Goss version

SOUTHAMPTON, HAMPSHIRE

38 Tudor House

The Tudor House was one of the best in Southampton when it was built in the fifteenth century by a wealthy local man, John Dawtry. It was constructed on the foundations of earlier houses which are now cellars, and incorporated shops facing on to St Michael's Square.

Now a museum, the house was known as the Palace House at the turn of the century and is still splendid today. All the timbers have been burnished by time to a rich patina, particularly in the hall where the old ceiling and minstrel's gallery make an ideal setting for the fine items on display.

The grounds include an Elizabethan knot garden as well as the stone shell of an extraordinarily well-preserved twelfth century town house. The text on the back of the model (not always accurate, however) reads: 'Tudor House, built 1535'. Tradition associates it with two royal visits. Henry VIII is alleged to have stayed there with Anne Boleyn, while Philip of Spain is supposed to have lodged there during his three day sojourn in Southampton in July 1554, prior to his marriage to Queen Mary at Winchester. However these legends cannot be confirmed.

The model, a beautiful copy by Goss, measures 7.5cm long at the base, 6.1cm deep and 6.6cm to the top of its vulnerable chimney.

**STOKE-ON-TRENT
STAFFORDSHIRE**

39 The Goss Oven

The model of the building known as the Goss Oven has only one firing oven (indicated by one chimney), while the existing building, in which the potter fired his later wares, has two. These ovens were constructed to keep pace with the firm's expansion and replaced a nineteenth-century bottle oven on which Goss probably based his model. He produced his first 'cottages' in 1893, and, as all his cottages, with very few exceptions, were accurate replicas, we can assume that this too was a faithful replica of a Goss oven of the time.

The present bottle oven in Sturgess Street with the two chimneys was probably built in 1905 and was known as the Old Falcon Pottery. It was taken over by Cauldon and closed down in the Second World War. The stages in the production work were as follows: the wet shaped clay was placed on saggers (6 inch deep earthenware trays), subjected to intense heat and then withdrawn, cooled and taken to the second floor of the large main building opposite where artists painted, decorated and glazed the models. Finally they were refired before packaging and despatch. The building was scheduled for demolition in 1986, but interest by Goss collectors and local residents has led to the building being listed for preservation. It is now owned by the Portmeirion Factory and has been restored as it was becoming dangerous. Stoke Corporation honoured the building with a blue plaque in 1995 stating: "The Kiln of the Falcon Pottery founded by W H Goss 1858", with in smaller letters underneath "Goss Collectors Club 1995".

There are two versions of this cottage with its single chimney – one brown, the other orange. Their size are the same at 7.6cm long, 4.5cm deep and 7.6cm high. Both come glazed or unglazed and occasionally bear a crest.

STRATFORD-UPON-AVON WARWICKSHIRE

40 Ann Hathaway's Cottage and
41 Shakespeare's Birthplace

Although Stratford-upon-Avon is still essentially a market town, its greatest industry is tourism, centred on the life and works of William Shakespeare (1564-1616). The Royal Shakespeare Theatre dominates the riverside and the lovely old streets are dotted with hallowed buildings: Shakespeare's birthplace; Ann Hathaway's cottage; Hall's Croft (John Hall was Shakespeare's son-in-law); the site of New Place, where Shakespeare retired, and the home of his mother, Mary Arden, some four miles away at Wilmcote. Harvard House (N0. 92) and Mason Croft (No. 93) may also be seen in Stratford-upon-Avon.

At only 18, Shakespeare married 26-year old Ann Hathaway, but went to London to launch his career, leaving his wife and three children behind. After great success as actor, poet and playwright, he returned to Stratford in 1610 to live as a country gentleman in New Place until his death. Ann died seven years later in 1623.

Ann Hathaway's cottage
Situated outside Stratford at Shottery, the cottage is of a similar date and construction, although the central chimney stack was rebuilt in 1697 by John Hathaway. It has a high-pitched thatched roof and 'crook' oak carved timbers which point to the fact that it was a farm house. Both properties are beautifully maintained inside and out and effectively furnished in period style.

Many potteries produced numerous models of both cottages. The Goss versions of Ann Hathaway's do not exactly reflect the actual features of the real building which is on two levels, the part furthest from the road being omitted on the model. One Goss version measures 6.2cm long, 3cm deep and 4.3cm high, while the model by Goss England is 10.9cm long, 5.5cm deep and 7.8cm high. A lovely W H Goss England 'Cottage Pottery' version, with, on some examples we have seen, the latter two words crossed through, is very interesting. Not only is

it rare but it has the famous Cottage Pottery colour, character and glaze. It measures 7.5cm long, 3.7cm deep and 5.2cm high.

Taylor & Kent made three models said to be 5cm, 7cm and 11.5cm long, while Willow Art had versions in lengths of 4.8cm, 5cm, 6.5cm, 10.9cm and 12.8cm. Hewitt & Leadbeater produced the largest we have seen at 21.5cm long, 10.4cm deep and 15.6cm high. A lovely Royal Doulton model is dated 1927 and, at 18.5cm long shows the entire length of the cottage in great detail.

Goss also produced a night-light model of Ann Hathaway's cottage at 15cm long, 8.2cm deep and 10.2cm high. In common with all but one of the Goss night-lights, it has a hole in the back for the candle and a round hole in the roof.

Shakespeare's birthplace
This house was built in about 1500 and divided into two sections, part residence, part quarters for his father's glove business. It is made of local materials with stone foundation walls and oak framing from the forest of Arden, infilled with wattle and daub, a substantial stone chimney stack and a tile roof. (It now has an annex at the back which is not shown on Goss or other models of the same period).

Models - Ann Hathaway's cottage

Goss

Doulton

Wilton, including one with ashtray

Goss night-light

'Cottage Pottery' mark

Goss England 'Cottage Pottery'

Models - William Shakespeare's cottage

Goss night-light

Goss

Unmarked

Taylor & Kent

Goss small

Copeland

Goss separate base

Goss solid base

*Willow Ann
Hathaway versions*

Two nightlight versions exist of Shakespeare's House. The larger is 18.2 cm long, 7.2cm deep and 9.2cm high, while the more unusual earlier 1893 version is in two pieces with a base and lid. The base is 11cm by 9.5cm, while the top measures 8.4cm long, 7cm deep and 9cm high.

Other Goss models of Shakespeare's house are 6.8cm long, 7.9cm long and 11cm long, with the largest apparently 14cm long. A so-called half-length model associated with the two-piece night-light but with a fixed base is 7.1cm long, 6cm deep and 8cm high. There are two varieties of this last model – one with a closed door and one with an open door.

Other makers of Shakespeare's house include Copeland, who in 1847 made what may be the forerunner of all the model cottages (see introduction). It is larger but fairly similar to Goss' two piece nightlight, although significant differences exist – no window in the roof, a plaque outside reading "The immortal Shakespeare was born in this house", a walkway and garden which form part of the base, the groove in which the Goss top sits is here a

ridge, there is an open window at ground floor. The base of the Copeland model is 13.2cm x 13.4cm, while the cottage is 11.6cm long, 9.6cm deep and 11.8cm high.

Following Copeland and Goss, Willow Art, Arcadian, Taylor & Kent and Leadbeater Art have also modelled Shakespeare's House, the most popular of all the miniature cottages. We know of four Willow sizes. The largest is 21cm long, 8.2cm deep and 10.8cm high, descending through a middle size of 13.1cm long, 5.2cm deep and 6.5cm high, a small model 6.5cm long, 3cm deep and 3.9cm high and the smallest at 4.8cm long. The Arcadian model is also small at 5cm long, 2.3cm deep and 3.1cm high, while the Taylor & Kent and Hewitt & Leadbeater models are 13.7cm long, 5.4cm deep and 7cm high and 15.4cm long, 6cm deep x 8.3cm high respectively. A rather crude Leadbeater model is 11 cm long, 4.5cm deep and 5.5cm high. There is an attractive foreign copy of the two-piece cottage which is 0.5cm shorter than the Goss prototype at 10.4 cm long. Distinguishing features are the lack of a Goss mark and no hole in the roof.

*Willow versions of
Shakespeare cottages*

SULGRAVE MANOR (about 8 miles from Banbury), of special interest as the home of the Ancestors of George Washington, first President of the United States.

SULGRAVE, NORTHAMPTONSHIRE

42 Sulgrave Manor

Sulgrave Manor, situated some 12 miles southwest of Northampton, is a lovely small manor house built of local limestone and oak in about 1500, by ancestors of George Washington, one of whom migrated to Virginia in 1656. Washington was, of course, the commander-in-chief in the War of Independence (1775-83) and the first president of the United States.

In 1914, to celebrate the centenary of the Treaty of Ghent which ended the War of 1812 (the final hostility between the United States and Great Britain) money was raised by private subscription to buy Sulgrave Manor. But plans to restore it had to be postponed because of the outbreak of World War I. After the armistice, with further funds from British and American contributors, restoration and refurnishing were completed. Both the Stars and Stripes and the Union Jack fly in the grounds, signifying the friendship between the two nations. The house itself appears bleak but inside the warmth and care given to the rooms and old furniture, especially that in the kitchen makes it a place of great interest.

The Goss model, measuring 12.7cm long by 6.8cm deep and 6.3m high, was probably produced to commemorate the 1814 treaty. It is extremely rare and has vulnerable chimneys.

Ellen Terry's Farm, Small Hythe.

TENTERDEN, KENT

43 Ellen Terry's Farmhouse

This lovely timbered house at Smallhythe near Tenterden dates from the fifteenth century, and is red-bricked with a tiled roof. It was the home of the distinguished actress, Dame Ellen Terry (1847-1928) who died here at the age of 81.

Ellen Terry was a gifted child actress being the daughter of actors and one of 11 children. She became the leading lady of Sir Henry Irving in many of Shakespeare's plays. She lectured in England, America and Australia on Shakespearean subjects, and was mother to actor, designer and producer, Edward Gordon Craig.

The house, which contains a wealth of stage memorabilia, is owned by the National Trust and is open to the public. It now has only two chimneys having lost one during rebuilding.

Goss' model which has three chimneys is 7.3cm long, 4.7cm deep at the base and approximately 4.9cm to the top of the least vulnerable chimney.

PART TWO
COTTAGES BY OTHER MANUFACTURERS

OTHER POTTERIES

There are over 200 potteries which have produced china that is collected today – some of course being more famous than others. Many produced 'cottages' or buildings but very few made coloured buildings. Among the latter those by Goss are the most famous and popular.

The best known of the non-Goss coloured 'cottage' producers are probably Willow and Arcadian followed by Carlton, Leadbeater and Grafton, and then Savoy, Podmore, Swan, Taylor & Kent, Tuscan and the earliest, Copeland (see Goss for reference to this important and huge factory). There are also a number of unmarked (cottages) of British and continental manufacture.

Arcadian China

The trade name used by Arkinsall & Sons Ltd, Arcadian Works, Stoke-on-Trent. The company was the biggest producers in Britain of crested china over the longest period and was the only one formed for the sole purpose of producing such china. The firm was founded in 1903 by Harold Taylor Robinson, who had begun his career as a traveller for Wiltshaw & Robinson (Carlton China) four years earlier. It is said that he founded the Arcadian China Company from his savings of £1,500 made during this period, no easy task in those days.

The firm continued production for the next 30 years and during this period bought out many firms, several of their dealings being unscrupulous and questionable. In 1920 Harold Taylor Robinson bought Cauldon Ltd for £100,000 and amalgamated most of the potteries he already owned and those in which he had a controlling interest under the new company.

Willow Art and Willow China

This company started up in about 1905 when Hewitt & Leadbeater joined in partnership. The firm produced various china novelties but 'Heraldic Ware' was one of the firm's leading lines. When the 1914 war started they produced wartime novelties but their real speciality was coloured buildings – these sold very cheaply at the time but are now becoming very rare and are much sought after by collectors. In 1919 Edwin Leadbeater left the firm to start a pottery on his own (Leadbeater Art China) which resulted in Mr Hewitt taking his brother into partnership and the firm became known as 'Hewitt Bros', while still using the Willow trade name. Unfortunately they did not survive the Depression possibly because they only produced novelties which were the last thing people could afford in those times. The firm was bought by Mr Harold Taylor Robinson in 1925 and almost immediately became a part of the Cauldon group. The Willow mark was not used after 1930 but the Willow moulds were being used after this date, as some recognisable Willow buildings are found marked Goss England – John Knox's House being such a model.

Podmore China

The trademark used by Podmore China Co., Elm St. Hanley, which came into being in 1921 and continued until 1941 when it became Sylvan Pottery Ltd. They produced crested china miniatures until the middle to late 20s with their models being on the large and heavy side. There is only one coloured 'cottage' so far known. This was produced in two sizes to represent the Bell Hotel, Tewkesbury, the home of Abel Fletcher in *John Halifax, Gentleman*.

Swan China

The trademark used by Charles Ford, of Cannon St Hanley. The original firm was founded in 1854 as T & C Ford. Then in 1871 it was known as Thomas Ford and in 1874 it became Charles Ford. The production of crested china seems to have started at the turn of the 20th century and in 1904 Mr Harold Taylor Robinson gained control of the firm. In 1910 it was made a branch of J A Robinson & Sons Ltd and production of Swan China was moved to Arcadian Works. The moulds were used by both Swan and Arcadian and some pieces have both marks. The Swan mark does not appear to have been used after 1925. The only coloured 'cottage' so far recorded is that of Shakespeare's House.

Tuscan China

Trademark used by R H. & S L Plant (Ltd), Tuscan Works, Longton. The company was founded in 1880 and when R H Plant died the business continued with his two sons and brother being in control.

The company is still in existence today surviving the depression and two World Wars, by following the trends and vagaries of public demand, producing Heraldic China, Ivory Porcelain or whatever was popular during each period. Tuscan China is quite fine and well produced but not too imaginative. The only cottage known at this time is the Look-Out House, Newquay.

Carlton China

A trademark used by Wiltshaw & Robinson Ltd, Carlton Works, Stoke-on-Trent, who started manufacturing china in 1890 making all types of fancy goods. In 1902 they started producing and advertising 'Carlton Heraldic China', probably the first of the Goss competitors. They used their own artists and produced many unusual and unique models. By 1920 they had come up with the Carlton Speciality – lustre ware which was used on most of their wares including some heraldic china. In 1931 they were placed in the hands of the Receiver, but it was possibly a voluntary liquidation which made it possible for another company to be formed and the firm merged with Savoy China. The merged firm continued to use both trademarks for some years. Carlton Ware was still being manufactured under the Carlton Ware Ltd trademark until the Autumn of 1992 when the production of

Carlton Ware ceased.

There are many coloured Carlton cottages. One which we decided not to include is Tintern Abbey in Chepstow as it was felt that its colouring was borderline between white and coloured cottages.

Wilton China

The trademark of A G Harley Jones at Wilton Pottery, Fenton which was started in 1905 and continued until 1934 when he became bankrupt. The firm was quite successful until 1920 after which time he expanded his business and extended his premises, by possibly borrowing money. However, turnover did not keep pace with his expansion and, although his models were original, he joined the crested china bandwagon too late to survive.

The only recorded cottages are Feathers Hotel, Ludlow, Shakespeare's House and Ann Hathaway's Cottage.

Savoy China

This was a trademark used by Birks, Rawlins & Co. (Ltd), Vine Pottery, Stoke. The firm was founded in 1900 and produced heraldic china in competition with Goss. They also produced miniature architectural models to order, although only Exeter Cathedral has been found. The other 'coloured cottage' so far known to have been produced by Savoy China is 'The Tumbledown Cottage', which is not thought to have been modelled on any particular building. It is of a fine china, beautifully modelled and coloured. The firm was placed in the hands of the Receiver in 1931 but was withdrawn when it merged with the makers of Carlton China and continued to use the Savoy trademark for a short time.

Taylor & Kent

The trademark used by Taylor & Kent (Ltd), Florence Works, Longton was just for the coloured buildings produced by them. These were of a finer china than their other wares which were marked Florentine China. The firm was another of the few to survive the depression in spite of losing one of the founders in the First World War. The two models of Ann Hathaway's Cottage and Shakespeare's

House were probably made before the Great War, whilst some are believed to have been made after 1930 and have a slightly different mark and a new trade name.

Grafton China

A trademark of Alfred B Jones & Sons Ltd, of the Grafton China Works, Longton, Staffs. The firm was founded in 1900 when A B Jones took his two sons in junior partnership with him. He produced all types of china and was possibly one of the better producers of fine china and competitors of Goss. They are one of the few firms which survived the depression, although most of their records were lost in a fire at the works in 1946. They have produced 'cottages' since 1945 but these are marked Royal Grafton. Those known to belong to the souvenir era between 1900 and 1939 are Captain Cook's House, Great Ayton; Couch's House, Polperro; the House on the Props, Polperro; Old Chapel, Lantern Hill, Ilfracombe; Old Maids Cottage, Lee; the Old Toll Bar, Gretna Green, and the Bell Hotel, Tewkesbury. Another, partially coloured cottage is the Gynn Inn, Blackpool.

This was the trademark used by Edwin Leadbeater, Drewery Place, Commerce St , Longton when he started up on his own in 1919 to manufacture heraldic china and ivory porcelain. He was the son of the senior partner of the Robinson & Leadbeater (R & L) firm for whom he worked until 1905 when he went into partnership with his brother-in-law Mr Arthur Hewitt, the company becoming Willow Art & Willow China. Certain cottages are found with the letters 'H & L' and these relate to the firm of Hewitt & Leadbeater before they became Willow Art and Willow China. One such 'cottage' is Priory Church, Christchurch. This partnership lasted until 1919, when he decided to try on his own despite the limited capital of £300 and only one oven. Leadbeater Art China only lasted five years as he was not as good a potter as his competitors and a poor business man. The coloured cottages known to be produced by this firm are Shakespeare's House and Ann Hathaway's Cottage, The Tan House at Little Stretton; the Gate House at Stokesay Castle; Izaak Walton's Cottage, Shallowford, Staffs; the Old Market Hall, Church Stretton; Bonchurch, Isle of Wight and Burns' cottage, Ayr.

An 'Irish Cottage' by Leadbeater 11.5cm. wide needs a mention, although it is not included in the book. It is simply a normal coloured Ann Hathaway Cottage with a different name and is not modelled on a genuine Irish Cottage. Nevertheless, for a collector of Leadbeater cottages it would be an important variation.

UNKNOWN POTTERIES

Many potteries which produced cottages with no trademark and a number of good Unmarked Models have been found. Those so far recorded are:

> Old Falcon Tavern,
> Bidford-on-Avon
> Pump Room & Baths,
> Trefriw Wells

Some larger models of famous buildings in the following towns are listed in the text: Congleton, Evesham, Ledbury, Hereford, Lullington in Sussex, Market Harborough, Morpeth and Upleatham. Some other cottages are marked 'British Manufacture', whilst others are foreign, probably German. Examples are Perth – Fair Maid's House; Dunfermline – Andrew Carnegie's Birthplace; and Llangollen – Plas Newyd.

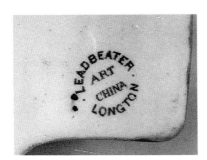

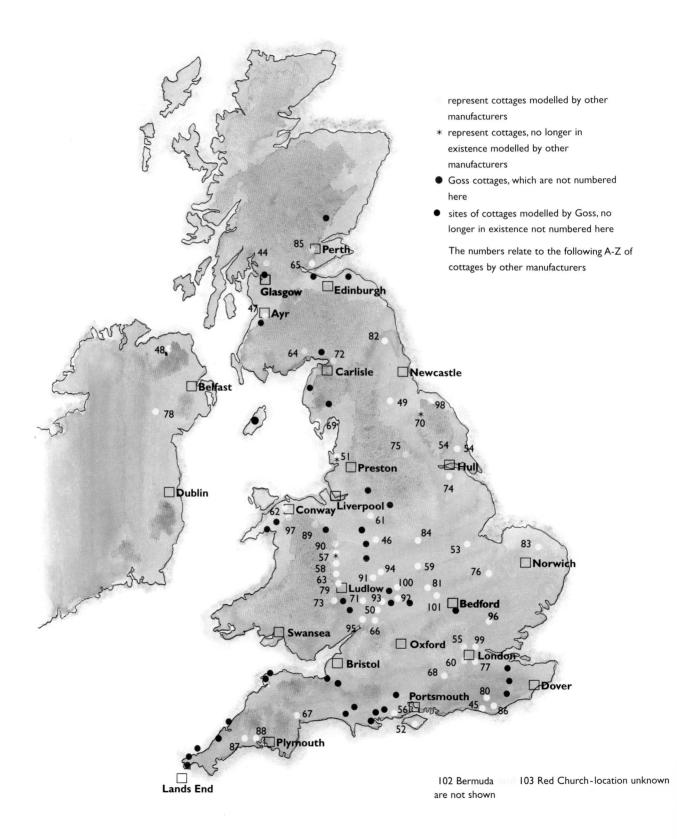

represent cottages modelled by other manufacturers

* represent cottages, no longer in existence modelled by other manufacturers

● Goss cottages, which are not numbered here

● sites of cottages modelled by Goss, no longer in existence not numbered here

The numbers relate to the following A-Z of cottages by other manufacturers

85 Perth
44
65
Glasgow
Edinburgh
47 Ayr

48
Belfast
78
82
64 72
Carlisle Newcastle
49 98
*70
69
75
54 54
*51
Preston Hull
74
62 Conway Liverpool
61
97 89
90 46 84
57 * 53 83
58 59 Norwich
63 94 76
79 91 100 81
73 Ludlow 71 93 92 101 Bedford
50 96
95
Swansea 66 55 99
Oxford London
60 77
68 80
Bristol 45 86
Portsmouth
67 56 52
88
87 Plymouth
Dublin

Lands End

102 Bermuda   103 Red Church-location unknown
are not shown

COTTAGES BY OTHER MANUFACTURERS

(These refer to the numbers on the map)

44 *Aberfoyle, Scotland*
Jean MacAlpine's Inn

45 *Alfriston, Sussex*
Old Star Inn

46 *Alton, Staffordshire*
The Round House

47 *Ayr, Scotland*
Tam O'Shanter Inn

48 *Ballymoney, Co. Antrim
Northern Ireland*
President McKinley's
Ancestral Home

49 *Barnard Castle
Co. Durham*
Blagrove House

50 *Bidford-on-Avon
Warwickshire*
Old Falcon Tavern

51 *Blackpool, Lancashire*
Gynn Inn

52 *Bonchurch
Isle of Wight*
Old Church

53 *Bourne, Lincolnshire*
Red Hall

54 *Bridlington, Yorkshire*
Priory Church

55 *Chalfont St Giles
Buckinghamshire*
Milton's Cottage

56 *Christchurch, Hants*
Priory Church

57 *Church Stretton
Shropshire*
Old Market Hall

58 *Church Stretton
Shropshire*
Tan House (Little
Stretton)

59 *Coalville
Leicestershire*
St Bernard's Monastry

60 *Colnbrook
Buckinghamshire*
The Ostrich Inn

61 *Congleton, Cheshire*
Moreton Old Hall

62 *Conwy, Wales*
Plas Mawr

63 *Craven Arms, Shropshire*
Gatehouse, Stokesay
Castle

64 *Dumfries, Scotland*
Burns House

65 *Dunfermline, Scotland*
Andrew Carnegie's
Birthplace

66 *Evesham
Gloucestershire*
Abbot Reginalds
Gateway & Vicarage

67 *Exeter, Devon*
Exeter Cathedral

68 *Godalming, Surrey*
Old Town Hall

69 *Grange-over-Sands
Cumbria*
Clock Tower

70 *Great Ayton, Yorkshire*
Captain Cook's House
(Melbourne)

71 *Great Malvern
Worcestershire*
St Ann's Well

72 *Gretna Green, Scotland*
Old Blacksmiths Shop
& Marriage Room

73 *Hereford, Herefordshire*
The Old House

74 *Hull, Yorkshire*
Wilberforce Museum

75 *Knaresborough
Yorkshire*
Ye Oldest Chymists
Shoppe in England

76 *Littleport
Cambridgeshire*
T & G W Union
Convalescent Home

77 *London*
The Old Curiosity
Shop

78 *Loughgall, Co. Armagh
Northern Ireland*
Dan Winter's Cottage

79 *Ludlow, Shropshire*
The Feathers Hotel

80 *Lullington, Sussex*
Lullington Church

81 *Market Harborough
Leicestershire*
Old Grammar School

82 *Morpeth
Northumberland*
Morpeth Castle
Gatehouse

83 *Norfolk Broads
Norfolk*
St Benet's Abbey

84 *Nottingham
Nottinghamshire*
Ye Olde 'Trip to
Jerusalem' Inn
1199 AD

85 *Perth, Scotland*
Fair Maid's House

86 *Pevensey, Sussex*
Old Mint House

87 *Polperro, Cornwall*
Couch's House

88 *Polperro, Cornwall*
House on the Props

89 *Ruthin, Clwyd, Wales*
Dean Goodmans
Birthplace

90 *Shrewsbury, Shropshire*
Irelands Mansion

91 *Stourbridge
West Midlands*
Dick Whittington Inn

92 *Stratford-on-Avon
Warwickshire*
The Harvard House

93 *Stratford-on-Avon
Warwickshire*
Mason Croft

94 *Sutton Coldfield
West Midlands*
Sutton Park
Druids Well

95 *Tewkesbury
Worcestershire*
Bell Hotel

96 *Thaxted, Essex*
The Guildhall

97 *Trefriw, Gwynedd
Wales*
Trefriw Chalybeate
Wells

98 *Upleatham*
Cleveland Church

99 *Waltham Abbey, Essex*
Waltham Abbey Tower

100 *Warwick, Warwickshire*
Leycester Hospital

101 *Wellingborough
Northants*
Old Tudor House

102 *Bermuda*
A Bermuda Cottage

103 Red Church
Location unknown

Rarity index to coloured cottages by manufacturers other than Goss

Notes A+ = extremely rare, D- = most numerous.

Aberfoyle Jean MacAlpine's Inn - Arcadian	A+
Bourne Red Hall - Willow	A+
Chalfont St Giles Milton's Cottage - Willow	A+
Congleton Moreton Hall - Unknown	A+
Dunfermline Andrew Carnegie's Birthplace - Willow	A+
Hull Wilberforce Museum - Willow	A+
Market Harborough Old Grammar School (2) - Unknown	A+
Morpeth Castle Gatehouse-Unknown	A+
Norfolk Broads St Benets Abbey - Willow	A+
Waltham Abbey Tower - Willow	A+
Alfriston Old Star Inn - Arcadian	A
Bedford Bunyan's - Willow	A
Church Stretton, Market Hall (2) – Leadbeater	A
Hereford Old House - Unknown	A
Kirriemuir A Window in Thrums - Carlton	A
Land's End First & Last House without annex - Arcadian	A
Ludlow Feathers (2) - Unknown	A
Upleatham Upleatham Church - Unknown	A
Wellingborough Old Tudor House - Arcadian	A
Alton Round House - Arcadian	A-
Barnard Castle Blagrove House - Hewitt & Leadbeater	A-
Buxton Cat and Fiddle - Kensington	A-
Colnbrook Ostrich Inn Willow and Unmarked	A-
Grange-Over-Sands Clock Tower - Carlton	A

Lullington Lullington Church - Unknown	A-
Stratford-on-Avon Shakespeare's House - Copeland	A-
Bermuda Bermuda Cottage - Unknown	B+
Conwy Plas Mawr - Unknown	B+
Craven Arms Stokesay Gate House - Leadbeater	B+
Great Ayton Captain Cook's House - Grafton	B+
Stratford-on-Avon Harvard House - Willow	B+
Trefriw, Gwynedd, Wales Trefriw Wells - Unknown	B+
Ayr Burns Cottage - Leadbeater	B
Gretna Green Blacksmith's Shop (6.0cm wide) - Willow	B
Isle of Man Pete's Cottage - Unknown	B
Littleport T.G.W.U. - Carlton	B
Polperro House on the Props - Grafton	B
Ruthin Dean Goodman's Birthplace - Arcadian	B
Bidford-on-Avon Falcon Tavern - Unknown	B-
Blackpool The Gynn Inn - Grafton	B
Ledbury Old Market - House Unknown	B
Ludlow Feathers Hotel - Willow	B
Shrewsbury Ireland's Mansion - Unknown	B-
Stourbridge Whittington Inn - Willow	B-
Thaxted Guildhall - Arcadian	B-
Ayr Tam o'Shanter - Unknown	C+
Bonchurch, Isle of Wight, Church - Leadbeater	C+

Exeter Exeter Cathedral - Savoy	C+
Ilfracombe St Nicholas Chapel - Willow	C+
Shallowford Izaak Walton – Leadbeater	C+
Sutton Coldfield Druids Well - Willow	C+
Upleatham Upleatham Church - Willow	C+
Warwick Leycester Hospital - Willow	C+
Ayr Burns' Cottage (2) - Arcadian	C
Ayr Burns' Cottage - middle size (9.7cm) - Willow	C
Ballymoney Northern Ireland McKinley's Ancestors Home - Unknown	C
Coalville St Bernard's Monastery - Willow	C
Craven Arms	C
Stokesay Stokesay Gate House - Willow	C
Evesham Abbot Reginald's Gateway & Vicarage - Unknown	C
Great Malvern St Ann's Well - Willow	C
Nottingham Ye Olde 'Trip to Jerusalem' Inn AD 1199 - Willow	C
Pevensey Old Mint House - Willow	C
Polperro Couch's House - Grafton	C
Bridlington Bridlington Priory - Arcadian	C
Church Stretton Tan House - Leadbeater and Willow	C-
Ilfracombe Old Maid's Cottage - Grafton	C-
Knaresborough Old Chymist's Shop - Carlton	C-
Lands End First and Last House with annex (2) - Arcadian	C-

Newquay Look-out House - Tuscan	C-
Ayr Burns' Cottage - Thistle	D+
Christchurch Priory Church - Hewitt & Leadbeater	D
Edinburgh John Knox - Willow	D+
Godalming Old Town Hall - Willow	D+
Grasmere Wordsworth's House - Carlton	D+
Gretna Green Toll Bar - Grafton	D+
Loughgall, Northern Ireland Dan Winter's Home - Unknown	D+
Perth Fair Maid's House (2) - Unknown	D+
Dumfries Burns House (2) – Willow	D
Ilfracombe Old Maids' Cottage - Willow	D
Ilfracombe St Nicholas Chapel - Grafton	D
Llangollen Plas Newyd - Unknown	D
London Old Curiosity Shop - Willow	D
Ludlow Feathers Hotel - Wilton	D
Stratford-on-Avon Masons Croft (3) - Hewitt & Leadbeater	D
Ayr Burns' Cottage - Willow	D-
Dunfermline Andrew Carnegie's Birthplace - Unknown	D-
Gretna Green Blacksmith's Shop - Many makers	D-
Tewkesbury Bell Hotel - Many makers	D-
Ann Hathaway - Many makers	D-
Shakespeare - Many makers	D-

ABERFOYLE, SCOTLAND

44 Jean MacAlpine's Inn

This cottage, now rebuilt, is located at Milton near Aberfoyle, north of Glasgow, in the middle of Rob Roy Country.

In 1817 Sir Walter Scott wrote *Rob Roy*, the story of a legendary highland freebooter – a Scottish Robin Hood – a drover and intriguer who helps his friends against the English during the 1715 Jacobite uprising. Jean MacAlpine's Inn fits into the story in only a small way as, according to the wording on the model cottage base, it is "the scene where a fray between Bailie Nicol Jarvie and the Highlanders took place." Scott described it thus:

> "From all we could see, Mrs MacAlpine's house, miserable as were the quarters it afforded, was still by far the best in the hamlet; and I dare say . . . you will hardly find it much improved at the present day, for the Scotch are not a people who speedily admit innovation, even when it comes in the shape of improvement."

The inn probably existed in 1715 and may be as early as 1665. It would have been visited by Scott in 1815 and featured in a film made about 1913 apparently starring Ellen McGregor, as well as in the 1922 film of Rob Roy.

The cottage represents two sections of a group of four sections in all. Built of large grey stones, it was variously thatched with juniper, broom and bracken and has a flagstone floor. The only smoke outlets are two small square wooden chimneys at each end of the dwelling, there being no chimney breasts, only hanging lums (*lums* being Scottish for chimney breast).

The site overlooks the River Forth, Forestry Commission firs and the main B829, from which the Clachan was at one time sign posted with steps rising some 25 feet to the site.

Jimmy Wright, the last occupant of Jean MacAlpine's Inn is said to have died in 1920 at the age of 92 paying 10/- rent per year (or approximately 1p per week). He had been a stone breaker/knapper, a roadworker, and a breeder of Scottish terriers. According to the locals, in the past if you wanted change of a £5

McKerracher's Cuddy at Jimmy Wrights

note Jimmy Wright would be sure to have it. Between 1920 and the late 1980s, the clachan only had sheep as its occupants and became derelict until the authors, ably assisted by many friends, restored it to its former state.

Modelled by Arcadian and later sold by Goss England at the 1938 Glasgow Exhibition as "An Clachan Cottage" it measures 10.5cm wide, 5.4cm deep and 5.4cm to top of chimney. It is very rare.

ALFRISTON, SUSSEX

45 Old Star Inn

The carving among the oak beams on the outside of this old inn are said by some to indicate that it was built early in the fifteenth century and by others to show that it might even date from some 200 years earlier. It may have been built as a religious house, associated with Battle Abbey, for the use of pilgrims on their way to the shrine of St Richard at Chichester.

A Dutch ship wrecked in the seventeenth century supplied the figurehead, which is now painted red. Other carvings are much earlier and have also been picked out in colour, much as they would have been when the inn was first built.

To us the most outstanding feature is the roof which is constructed of Horsham stone and set on heavy oak to support the great bulk of each stone – about half a hundredweight. The building has fine old oak features inside, as well. It has been enlarged to cope with modern needs as it is now a large hotel.

The model, only by Arcadian, is 10.4cm long, 5.9cm deep and 8.6cm high.

ALTON, STAFFORDSHIRE

46 Round House

Alton is a wonderful old town on the edge of the Derbyshire Peak District National Park with the first recorded mention of it dating to 716 AD Today it is probably best known for the Alton Towers Amusement Park.

The Round House, or local lock-up, stands amongst other lovely old buildings in Old Alton. It was built in 1830 by the Earl of Shrewsbury to house drunks and felons awaiting trial by a circuit judge at the local Assizes. Inside the building, smooth walls with no footholds, an earthen floor on a rock base with a drainage hole and an iron bed with a missing leg provided the facilities for the reluctant 'guests'. Originally the walls were blackened with smoke, not least because one of the inmates set fire to straw bedding using the fire as an excuse to escape. When the door was opened he ran to Farley, the next village, believing, incorrectly, that he could in that way escape the jurisdiction of the local constabulary.

In the 1930s the building was used as a butcher's shop as it provided a cool storage for meat. During the Second World War it was used to store waste paper and aluminium collected for the war effort. It is now in the care of the local council but is not used for any specific purpose.

The model by Arcadian has no windows and is brown in colour. It has the words "Round House, Alton" written below the heavy door and measures 4.8cm in diameter and 8.4cm high.

AYR, SCOTLAND

47 Tam o' Shanter Inn

Ayr has been a settlement for over 1000 years, its location at the mouth of the river Ayr providing a natural harbour, reaching a peak of prosperity between the twelfth to sixteenth centuries when the burgh (borough) was third in importance to Leith and Dundee in Scotland.

The Tam o' Shanter Inn dates from 1748 when it was a house built by James Shearer on the site of a delapidated older cottage. Later he became the first landlord around 1775, brewing his own ale in the back. Possibly Robert Burns drank there, although it was not so-called in those times, only acquiring its name from James Kerr following Burns' story in verse about Douglas Graham (Tam o' Shanter) and the witches. Andrew Glass, Innkeeper from 1857, used the association to make an ordinary pub into a famous landmark, a fame that has lasted to the present and kept the pub from destruction. Today the Inn belongs to the burgh, bought for £4,000 in 1943 and opened as a museum in 1957. It is currently being renovated.

The model, of unknown make, is unique in having 'Tam o'Shanter Inn' embossed in front below the thatch. It measures 9.1cm long, 6.4cm deep and 11.7cm high with an open base.

**BALLYMONEY, COUNTY ANTRIM
NORTHERN IRELAND**

48 President McKinley's Ancestral Home

William McKinley, the 25th President of the United States of America, was assassinated in 1901 during his second term of office, having become president for the first time in 1897. The first record of his ancestors is in Callander, Scotland in the sixteenth century. It was 1690 that the Irish connection was recorded when James, The Trooper, McKinley joined the English Army to fight at the Battle of the Boyne in Ireland. He stayed behind after the war and his family became established in Northern Ireland. The president's ancestors emigrated to America in the first half of the eighteenth century. Back in Ireland, Frank McKinley, grand uncle of the president, was executed by the English for his part with other townspeople of Ballymoney, in the 1789 insurrection.

Although the ancestral home was burnt down at this time, it was later restored. Known as Conagher farm, it bears a blue heritage plaque. Lying just off the Ballymoney-Dervoch road, it looks like an uninhabitable farm shed.

The unmarked model is most unusual. As with Dan Winter's Cottage at Loughgall (No. 78), it is a money box with a 3.2cm slot on the roof ridge for inserting pennies but with no aperture for their subsequent removal. In addition, it is unglazed except for the glazed plate below the front doors stating in gold its claim to fame – "Ancestral Home of President McKinley in Co. Antrim, Ireland" with three Shamrock leaves at the beginning and the end. The measurements are 12.5cm wide, 5.7cm deep and 8.1cm high.

BARNARD CASTLE
COUNTY DURHAM

49 Blagrove House

The history of Barnard Castle dates to prehistoric times with a Bronze Age barrow (burial mound) and a nearby Iron Age settlement. The castle was founded by Bernard de Balliol in about 1093 AD.

Blagraves House is the correct name of the house, which is called Blagrove House on the model. It is named after Binkes Blagrave who had rebuilt the house on its medieval foundations in the seventeenth century. At one time it was an inn called 'The Boar's Head' at which Oliver Cromwell is alleged to have dined in 1648.

The extensive, vaulted medieval cellars were traditionally used as dungeons and it is said that a passage leads either to the castle or to

Egglestone Abbey, but this has not yet been discovered. Later the cellars housed a brewery using well water to make the ale. Deeds of 1725 record that Blagroves was sold for £126.1s, provided that £1.14s a year was given to the poor. Today it is both a private home and a restaurant.

The words 'Blagrove House, Barnard Castle' are engraved on the front and rear of this model by Hewitt and Leadbeater, which was probably produced before 1920 at which time the statues that now adorn the front of the life-size building were installed yet do not appear on the model.

The model in our collection has been damaged in the left-hand corner where a second chimney may have been. The real building has a chimney in this position which belongs to the house next door. The model measures 15.4cm wide, 11.9cm deep and 18.4cm high.

THE OLD FALCON INN, BIDFORD.

BIDFORD-ON-AVON
WARWICKSHIRE

50 Old Falcon Tavern

Bidford-on-Avon goes back to Roman times, when nearby Icknield Way was a main thoroughfare. It got a market licence in 1220, and the eight-arch bridge was built in 1455.

The Falcon Tavern, opposite the market in the middle of town, was built in about 1530, of shaped Cotswold stone. Recent additions include brick chimneys and a red tiled roof. It has old windows of hand made glass and one stained-glass window celebrating William Shakespeare, who may have been a frequent visitor.

According to local legend, a group of drinkers, 'the toppers and sippers' of Bidford, challenged neighbouring Stratford, whose tipplers included Shakespeare, to a drinking bout. Shakespeare noted the event in verse:

"I have drunk at Piping-Pebworth,
Dancing Marston, Haunted Hillborough,
Hungry Grafton, Dodging Exhall,
Papist Wixford, Beggarly Broom
and Drunken Bidford."

Old postcards and a jubilee plate depict the tavern with the caption, 'Drunken Bidford'.

In 1754, the building became a police station and workhouse, was later an antiques shop, and has now been converted into flats, although the outside looks exactly the same. The only model we have seen, its maker unknown, has details on two sides, is unmarked and measures 10.5cm long, 4.4cm deep and 9.9cm high.

BLACKPOOL, LANCASHIRE

51 The Gynn Inn

Blackpool received its name from the peat-blackened stream which flows into the sea; the word 'gynn' means an opening or abyss, a road or passage down to the sea. It is said that an inn existed on this site as early as the 1500s, while records state that an Edward Bonny took it over after his marriage in 1741. Standing as it did on the North Shore, it has been suggested that the inn was used for smuggling. Whether it was or not, it was certainly one of the first inns to take visitors, later undercutting the other local inn by charging only 8d for a day's board and lodging as opposed to 10d.

In 1833 the Gynn Inn was responsible for saving a Scottish schooner or sloop from shipwreck during a June storm. By placing a light in the window, the vessel was able to steer safely up the gully, her bowsprit almost touching the door of the inn. By 1898 the Blackpool & Fleetwood tram road passed the inn's door with the Blackpool Promenade tramway arriving in 1900. When the Promenade was extended northwards in 1921, the old Gynn Inn was demolished much to the sorrow of many Blackpudlians. The last licensee, Mrs Alice Ashworth had been there for 40 years, the last 30 as a widow holding the licence herself.

The glazed Grafton model is white with a red roof. Emblazoned on the side nearest to the sea and the front of the building are the words 'Gynn Inn', while the base bears the inscription "the model of Blackpool's famous landmark the Old GYNN INN, demolished in 1921". The two characteristic Grafton holes are missing from the base of the model we have seen, which is 12.5cm wide, 6.7cm deep and 8.1cm high.

BONCHURCH, ISLE OF WIGHT

52 Old Church

In AD755, Monks from Normandy dedicated a building here to St Boniface, who had been martyred the previous year in Holland. This church, one of the smallest in the south of England, was built of local stone on the same site in about 1070, and rebuilt, in the thirteenth century. The porch and bellcote were added in 1830 and repairs were carried out between the two World Wars.

Gravestones in the churchyard date back to the seventeenth century and include that of William Adams, author of *Shadow of the Cross*

and other sacred allegories. Clearly this was a major attraction at the turn of the century referred to on many postcards. One adjacent house was home to Charles Dickens, who wrote part of *David Copperfield* there, while Algernon Swinburne, the poet, was born in the other adjoining house, East Dene.

The medieval murals are intact, as are ancient windows and woodwork, and the altar rail made from the original roof beams. Candlelit services are held on 5 June, St Boniface's day, and at other times during the summer.

The model is by Leadbeater and measures 11cm long, 4.4cm deep and 5.9cm high.

Red Hall, Bourne

BOURNE, LINCOLNSHIRE

53 Red Hall

Bourne pre-dates Roman times, but it began to flourish during the Roman occupation with the construction of Carr Dyke, which protects the low fen farms by draining water into the River Nene.

Red Hall, a handsome Tudor house of brick and stone was erected towards the end of the sixteenth century (possibly by Gilbert Fisher) on the double pile principle. It has four rooms on the ground floor comprising a hall, dining parlour, kitchen and buttery, four bedrooms upstairs and a lofty gallery and other rooms above.

Sir Everard Digby, executed as one of the chief conspirators in the Gunpowder Plot of 1605, lived here, and this may have been the place where the plot was actually hatched.

The estate was sold to the Bourne-Essendine Railway in 1860 and became an important railway junction when it was absorbed by the Great Northern Railway in 1864. Red Hall became the station master's house. After the railway closed, the building's future was in doubt, until it was bought by the Bourne United Charities, who restored it and opened it to the public in 1972.

The model by Willow Art has details on three sides, measures 8.3cm long, 6.7cm deep and 7cm high, and is extremely rare.

BRIDLINGTON, YORKSHIRE

54 Priory Church

This beautiful building, part of a monastery founded in about 1133 AD, escaped destruction at the time of Henry VIII's dissolution because it was used as a parish church. It was built on land formerly occupied by both Saxon and Norman churches.

When the monastery was dissolved in 1537, the prior and others were executed for insurrection, and all the buildings except this church and the gate-house were destroyed or abandoned to fall into disrepair. During general restoration work between 1846 and 1879, the western towers were remodelled, the four spirelets being raised to a height of 46 metres.

The model, by Arcadian, is beige and measures 3.7cm wide, 6.9cm deep and 6.4cm high.

CHALFONT ST GILES, BUCKINGHAMSHIRE

55 Milton's Cottage

This lovely cottage, covered in climbing plants and with a well-kept garden, was probably built at the end of the 16th century and is currently open to the public. The chimney and chimney breast by the roadside were never included as part of the model and at one time the building had a two storey porch which was pulled down between 1825 and 1830 because it was dangerous.

Many well known people have lived in the cottage, or part of it, among them a famous gunsmith named Truelock (mentioned in Pepys' diary) and Old Betty who owned a kitten with seven legs. John Milton (1608-1674) rented the house in 1665 when, being a Roundhead, he moved from London to escape both the plague and the Royalists. It was here that he finished his most famous work *Paradise Lost*.

Legend has it that an American wished to purchase the building and erect it in America, a plan which stimulated the British public to establish a Jubilee Fund to which Queen Victoria donated £20. In 1887 the cottage was purchased by the Milton Cottage Trust.

The well-proportioned Willow model was made before 1910, and measures 5.9cm wide, 2.8cm deep and 4.5cm high. The words 'John Milton's Cottage' are written on the back.

Christchurch Priory and Ruins, Bournemouth.

CHRISTCHURCH, HAMPSHIRE

56 Priory Church

During the reign of Alfred the Great, King of Wessex between the years 871 and 899, a series of fortified towns, or burhs, was established along the Hampshire coast as protection against invasion by the Danes. Even before that time, however, in about 700 AD Christians may have built a church at the settlement then known as Twynham.

The building of the Norman Priory began in about 1095, and it became so important that it gave its name, Christchurch, to the town. Monastic life continued peacefully until Henry VIII shut down the priory during the dissolution. But an unprecedented petition forced him to give it to the town rather than destroy it. Today the priory is little changed and still houses a carved stone head dating back to the 8th century.

The rare model, by Hewitt & Leadbeater, is heavy and set on a green base. It measures 22.2cm wide, 6.5cm deep and 10.6cm high. It is found in both glazed and partly glazed versions.

CHURCH STRETTON, SHROPSHIRE

57 Old Market Hall

The original market hall, built in 1671, stood near the centre of Church Stretton on what is now the square. It was destroyed by fire in 1839. Like the Ledbury market hall which was much smaller, it was built on stilts, had an open ground floor and three sets of interconnecting rooms above. It was replaced by a red brick market hall, with stone pillars, demolished in 1958 having become unsafe. Today the market square is empty.

The Leadbeater Art models are of the timbered building. They are rare but dull. The smaller version is apparently 9.5cm long with the other dimensions in scale, while the larger is 10.5cm long, 4.2cm deep and 7.3cm high.

CHURCH STRETTON, SHROPSHIRE

58 The Tan House (Little Stretton)

The Tan House at Little Stretton by Church Stretton nestles unobtrusively behind a holly hedge in rural surroundings. A picturesque Tudor building with bay windows, it was built between 1520 and 1620, and was originally the residence of the tannery manager.

It underwent internal changes during Victorian times, and contains a wealth of timber furnishings from old churches. One of the previous owners, Derwent Wood, was in the pottery business and would have known Goss and Leadbeater. His additions to the property were flamboyant and exciting and much admired by visitors. Today the house is a private residence, not open to the public.

There are two models, one by Leadbeater and one by Willow Art, identical in every way except for size. The Leadbeater version measures 10.8cm wide, 5.7cm deep and 7.1cm high, while the larger Willow model measures 12.5cm wide, 6.4cm deep and 8.5cm high.

Left: Willow. Right: Leadbeater

COALVILLE, LEICESTERSHIRE

59 St Bernard's Monastery

In 1835 – relatively recently in terms of the other cottages – Trappist monks laid the foundations for this lovely abbey which was designed, free of charge, by the leading Gothic-revival architect of the day, A W Pugin. Its construction was financed by the sixteenth Earl of Shrewsbury.

Opened in 1844, its fame grew as many rich and influential visitors came, including William Wordsworth and Florence Nightingale. Its main function was to serve the poor, including thousands of Irish immigrants escaping the potato famine. By the 1860s and 1870s some 70 monks were in residence. Although by 1910 the numbers of monks had declined, between the two World Wars their numbers increased again and numerous postcards were produced.

Unfortunately, the model, by Willow Art, is one of the least inspired of all the coloured china cottages and depicts only a small section of the building. It measures 10cm wide, 5.4cm deep and 10.3cm high.

COLNBROOK, BUCKINGHAMSHIRE

60 The Ostrich Inn

from the French *pieds poudreux*, meaning dusty-footed – which had summary powers over buyers and sellers who were there temporarily. However a few years later during the Civil War (1642-46) it lost its charter and reverted to village status.

In the 18th century the inn became a staging post on the road from London to Bristol and later achieved notoriety when an innkeeper named Jarman was alleged to have murdered some 60 people by tipping sleeping travellers into a cauldron of boiling water.

The inn externally is much as it was when rebuilt, except that a gallery at the back has almost totally disappeared. Inside, however, there have been many changes, including the addition of a seventeenth century staircase and panelling. But, with its black beams, it has retained its medieval atmosphere.

A rare model by Willow Art measures 9.2cm long, 4.7cm deep and 8cm high. Another, unmarked version, possibly also by Willow, is 9.1cm long, 4.2cm deep and 7.1cm high.

The Ostrich Inn is said to be the fourth oldest inn in the country, but records dating from 1106 suggest that it may actually be the oldest. During the Middle Ages it was often used by guests to change before arriving at Windsor Castle. It was rebuilt in 1500 of timber and plaster, with a red tiled roof and a projecting upper storey with gables at either end. A gateway, with gates dating from the rebuilding, leads to the old stable yard (now a car park).

In 1635, Colnbrook received a charter which included provision for a weekly market as well as for a 'pie powder' court which was held in the Ostrich Inn. These were wayfarers' courts –

CONGLETON, CHESHIRE

61 Moreton Old Hall

This is one of the most famous of all the timber-framed buildings in Britain and is now in the care of the National Trust.

The Moreton family were powerful local landlords from the thirteenth century onwards, serving as mayors of Congleton and tax collectors. They enlarged their estate by buying up land following the depopulation caused by the Black Death, the Dissolution of the Monasteries and the sale of Church Lands. They invested their wealth in the building of Moreton Hall which was begun around 1440, with extensions in the 1480s

and again in the early sixteenth century and the 1570s. It is on these later additions that the model is based being a copy of the South Wing and the Gate House. This part includes the oak-panelled 68 foot Long Gallery, a feature popular in big houses at that time and used for walking and indoor games.

The extremely rare model manages to combine solidity with much detail and intricate colouring. Although unmarked it is probably by Leadbeater and was expensive at the time, being marked with a pencilled 50/- on the back. The model measures 11.7cm wide, 8cm deep and 11.5cm high.

Banqueting Hall, Plas Mawr.

CONWAY.

**CONWY, GWYNEDD
NORTH WALES**

62 Plas Mawr

Plas Mawr, meaning Great Hall, occupies a congested site in the middle of Conwy which does not show it off to the full. Nevertheless the excellent stonework and beautiful interior with magnificent plasterwork can still be appreciated. The main building was completed around 1580 and the gatehouse, fronting the High Street, which is the subject of this model was probably added around 1585.

Conwy is certainly rich in history. Celtic hill forts were succeeded by the Romans. Then after their departure the area suffered attacks from the sea and the kingdom of Gwynedd was formed. The English Norman lords coveted Wales and the constant warring was unceasing until Edward I built Conway Castle and the city walls between 1283-1287 (a period when he also built Beaumaris Castle, Hawarden Castle and many others). By the 16th century the town was prosperous and it was then that the Wynnes build Plas Mawr. Apparently the ghost of Robert Wynne's first wife haunts the Lantern Room within the house.

The house now belongs to the Welsh Office and its future is uncertain, although a museum housing period furniture has been mooted. The unmarked model is by an unknown maker. It measures 9 cm wide, 5.2 cm deep and 9 cm high.

CRAVEN ARMS, SHROPSHIRE

63 Gatehouse Stokesay Castle

This picturesque, timbered gate-house, built at the beginning of the seventeenth century is decorated with carvings of Adam and Eve, the serpent and the forbidden fruit. It is the only part of Stokesay Castle that is occupied.

The name dates from William Conqueror's time when a dairy farm or 'stoke' was given to the Say family. The present moated building, one of the finest fortified manor houses in England, was built in about 1290 by a wealthy clothier, Lawrence de Ludlow, to combat threats from the Welsh border. It was garrisoned during the Civil War (1642-46) by Lord Craven, a royalist, but fell without a struggle and was undamaged.

It was then neglected until John Hallcroft, MP for Worcester, bought it in 1869 and restored it. It has not been fully occupied since.

The building was modelled by both Willow Art and Leadbeater Art. That by Willow Art measures, at base, approximately 11.6cm long, 5.3cm deep and 10.7cm high. The smaller Leadbeater Art model is approximately 10.4cm long, 4.9cm deep and 10.6cm to the top of the higher chimney.

Although at first glance similar in size and colouring, there are minor variations in the moulds. The leaded windows in the facade of the Willow Art model are inset and the roof extends along the gutter line below the gable window, features not apparent on the Leadbeater version. However, the latter does have a more detailed chimney and wood framework which make it distinctive.

Left: Willow Art. Above left: Leadbeater
Above right: Willow Art

**DUMFRIES
SCOTLAND**

64 Burns' House

Robert Burns moved to this house in Dumfries in May 1793. Having gained promotion as an exciseman and with it a rise in pay of £20 to £75 a year, he was able to afford this self-contained house with a rent of £8 a year. However, suffering from ill health, he died here only three years later on 21st July 1796 aged just 37.

Today it seems quite an ordinary house, but it must have been very desirable in the eighteenth century as it is built of well cut, local red sandstone and has a slate roof with two chimneys. The attractive window boxes – a feature of the china cottages – no longer exist; but like its more famous counterpart in Alloway, Ayr, the house is now a museum.

Models by Willow Art are very pretty – white with grey roof, green woodwork and colourful window boxes. The correct two-chimney version is 8.4cm wide, 5.3cm deep and 8.6cm high, whilst the slightly larger one-chimney version is 8.5cm wide, 5.5cm deep and 9.0cm high.

DUNFERMLINE, SCOTLAND

65 Andrew Carnegie's Birthplace

Dunfermline is north of Edinburgh on the other bank of the River Forth. In 1835 when the town's most famous son, Andrew Carnegie, was born, neither the railway nor road bridge existed. The Carnegie family lived in one of the attic rooms in the cottage in Moodie street, the downstairs being used for weaving. Andrew's father was a weaver of fine linen (damask) with first one and later four looms. At that time there was also an annex which formed a small shop, and this is the version similar to the early bisque model. The annex was removed for road improvements and the Willow model which shows a new window reflects this alteration.

In May 1848 when Andrew was 13, the impoverished family decided to join relatives in Pittsburgh, USA. Andrew began his later glittering career as a bobbin boy on $1.20 per week. By taking evening classes and using the library he soon progressed and at the age of 33 after the Civil War was earning $50,000 per annum. He was now independent and, through a combination of luck and judgement, his work in the iron making and railway business led him to become the richest man in America. However, despite his new found wealth, he never forgot his native Scotland, purchasing several properties there. Retiring early he endowed 3,000 libraries, 8,000 church organs and made many other charitable bequests.

The bisque model, made sometime before 1916, is by an unknown, possibly German, maker, and is similar to Perth's Fair Maid's House (No. 85) with outside steps. It measures 8.7 cm wide, 4.9 cm deep and 7.8 cm to the top of the chimney. The words the "Birthplace of Andrew Carnegie" are either on the gable end or above the doors.

The Willow Art model was produced later and is extremely rare. It measures 7.1 cm wide, 5.0 cm deep and 5.3 cm high.

Unknown manufacturer

Willow

EVESHAM, WORCESTERSHIRE

66 Abbot Reginald's Gateway and Vicarage

Between 1122 and 1149, Abbot Reginald, a monk of Gloucester, built the wall still known as Abbot Reginald's Wall. Today it surrounds the two churches of All Saints for the townsfolk and St Laurence's, the pilgrims church. In the twelfth century it contained the cemetery and the Abbey itself, built at the beginning of the eighth century. The latter were destroyed at the Dissolution after 1540, leaving only the two churches.

The contemporary Norman-style Abbot Reginald's Gateway, was originally much taller, but when the Abbey was destroyed, the footpath below was raised by approximately three feet and, in the sixteenth century, the Tudor vicarage was built alongside and over the gateway.

The town of Evesham, did not exist until the late seventh century when a swineherd named Eoves saw a vision of three maidens, one of whom was exceptionally beautiful. Eoves told Egwin who after fasting, praying and visiting the same spot, also saw the vision. As a result, a monastery was begun at the site in 702. Egwin became the first Abbot from 710 until his death in 717. The town was built around the monastery, and took its name from Eoves-Ham.

The rare model is by an unknown maker and measures 13cm wide, 6.2cm deep, and 9.3cm high. The three bollards, which were placed under the archway about 1910, are still in position and indicated in a crude manner.

EXETER, DEVONSHIRE

67 Exeter Cathedral

The ancient Norman cathedral with its two bulky towers stands in what was the ancient Roman city. In 1050, Edward the Confessor installed the first bishop to protect the many churches elsewhere in Devon and Cornwall. The building was begun in about 1112, only five years after the central tower of Winchester Cathedral had collapsed, which may account for the double towers. It was probably completed by 1160. Local sandstone from nearby Silverton was used in the construction, but it does not stand up well to wind and weather, and many repairs and replacements have had to be carried out over the centuries. The cathedral has elaborately carved oak decorations, a fine minstrels' gallery and a remarkable astronomical clock.

The model, by Savoy, measures 15cm deep, 8.7cm across its two towers and 7.4cm high.

GODALMING, SURREY

68 Old Town Hall

The Town Hall, a tiny, delightful building known as 'the pepper pot,' dates from 1814 and stands on the site of the original town hall which was built early in the fifteenth century, when Godalming was an important centre of the woollen trade. Until 1908, borough council meetings were held here; it is still the appointed place for official announcements such as royal proclamations, and it houses the museum of antiquities.

The ancient building had a clock on the north wall to assist the inhabitants in "the keeping of Fitt and Ordinary Hours for their Apprentices, Servants and Workmen." A bell in the turret was meant to warn of fire, but apparently it went unheeded, for the building burned down in 1780.

The replacement, for which money was raised by public subscription, is made of red brick covered with stucco plaster. The upper storey rests on arches, giving cover for a small market. A square turret houses the 'new' clock, which was made in 1815; the bell above dates from 1792.

The model is by Willow Art. It measures 9.7cm wide, 5.2cm deep and 10.5cm high. Our one bears the Godalming town crest.

GRANGE-OVER-SANDS, CUMBRIA

69 Clock tower

The Clock Tower was donated to Grange-over-Sands by Mrs Sophia Deardon at precisely 12 o' clock on 12th December 1912 (i.e. at 12 on 12.12.12.). It is made of local limestone, probably from the Eden Mount quarry, and sandstone from St Bees. The inscription over the door reads 'AMORIS DONUM'. As well as this project, Mrs Deardon also donated Yewbarrow Craggs to the people of Grange.

Records of Grange date back to 1598 when it was a small port, while in the early 1800s it was a fishing village, left behind by the Industrial Revolution. However, nicknamed the 'Torquay of the North', it became a popular wintering place.

Over the years, the sand has accumulated as a result of the changed course of the River Kent following the construction of a railway viaduct and causeway. Today it is hard to imagine that it was ever a port.

Many accounts tell of the dangers of the quick sands and the speed of the incoming tides. On one occasion a carriage returning from Manchester was trapped in quick sand. While the outside passengers jumped to safety, the Reverend Rigg was almost forgotten and had to be extricated with great difficulty through the window. Several months later, the coach reappeared having been washed up four or five miles along the shore. Rev. Rigg's bag and papers were still intact, if waterlogged, and were able to prove the validity of the legal transaction he had travelled to Manchester to execute! The colourful model by Carlton has a 6.2cm square base and is 16cm high.

GREAT AYTON, YORKSHIRE

70 Captain Cook's Cottage, now in Australia

One of the most visited buildings in Australia is James Cook's house (so-called), which was shipped to Melbourne, Victoria from Great Ayton in 1934 (in 235 cases and 40 barrels) as part of Victoria's centenary celebrations. Made of brick and stone, it was originally thatched, but now has a pantile roof which follows the original line.

It was built by Cook's parents in 1755 on a parcel of land fronting Goat Lane (now called Easby Lane). Cook (1728-1799) was 27 when it was built and probably never lived in it, although he probably visited in around 1771-72, his mother having died in 1768.

Captain Cook is noted chiefly for his round-the-world voyages on board Endeavour, beginning in 1769 during which he explored the coasts of Australia and New Zealand. Earlier he had been slightly involved in the capture of Quebec and also helped survey Nova Scotia and Newfoundland. In 1776 he left to attempt the discovery of a north-west passage from the Pacific, failing as no such passage existed. He did, however, rediscover the Sandwich Islands in Hawaii, where he was killed by natives on 14 February 1779.

Grafton produced this rare model after 1933, mainly for the Australian market. It has details on all sides and a caption stating that the house has been re-erected in Melbourne. It measures 9.6cm long, 7cm deep and 8.6cm high.

COLLECTING MINIATURE COTTAGES

**GREAT MALVERN
WORCESTERSHIRE**

71 St Ann's Well

St Ann's Well, on the slopes of the Worcestershire beacon, overlooks Great Malvern. The well has been known since medieval times, possibly as early as 1282. Records indicate that the cult of St Ann, mother of the Virgin Mary and the patroness of wells and springs, was at its height during the fourteenth century. Water from the area has been bottled since 1622.

By the mid-eighteenth century, Malvern waters had become widely known, principally through the efforts of one Dr John Wall, who praised them in print for being almost completely free of minerals. A comic wrote,

"The Malvern water," says Dr John Wall
"Is famed for containing just nothing at all."

A renewed surge of interest came when water cures became popular in the nineteenth century; a splendid pump room and baths being built here between 1815 and 1819. Distinguished visitors over many decades have allegedly included Queen Victoria, Florence Nightingale, Dickens, Carlyle, Darwin and Gladstone.

Despite the erstwhile fame of the Malvern waters, all of the handsome buildings have disappeared, and the well itself was threatened with demolition in 1963. It is now part house, part shop, part snack-bar.

The unglazed model, by Willow Art, is colourful and beautifully fashioned. It is 10.6cm wide, 5.5cm deep (maximum) and 6.2cm high.

72 Gretna Green, Scotland, the Old Blacksmith's Shop and Marriage Room
See Goss No 18, Gretna Green, the Old Toll Bar

HEREFORD

73 The Old House

The house, which exists today, has been altered considerably since it was built in what is believed to be 1621 when it was one of a pair of houses in Butchers Lane or 'The Butchery'.

It has an elaborately carved porch which includes the coat of arms of the Butchers Guild, indicating the importance of the building as the Butchers Guild had separate rooms in the Market Hall in Hereford. The house is three storeys high and is said to be an excellent specimen of Jacobean domestic architecture, being timber framed with wattle and daub infill.

Besides being a butchers it has had other uses and was a saddlery until 1872 when it became a

hardware shop and, still later, a wet fish shop. Eventually it was bought by the Worcester City and County Banking Company who were incorporated into Lloyds Bank. Maps of Hereford show a vacant site in 1610, but by 1757 the Old House is shown as one of a pair. In 1837 the house was left isolated as the adjacent building was pulled down. Other documentary evidence relating to the property is the will of Thomas Wheeler, a saddler, dated 1836. In 1928 Lloyds Bank presented the building to the city of Hereford and it became the museum it remains today, housing a collection of early oak furniture.

The maker of the model is unknown, although Leadbeater is a possibility. It measures 11.8 cm wide, 7.8 m deep and 12.0 cm high.

HULL, YORKSHIRE

74 The Wilberforce Museum

William Wilberforce was born in this house, overlooking the quay in Hull, in 1759. It had been built by John Lister in 1600 and King Charles I had stayed there in 1639. By 1709 the house was owned by the Thornton family who were in the export business. William Wilberforce was apprenticed to Thorntons and later married his master's daughter Sarah in 1711. Their grandson William, with whom we are concerned, was born in a first floor room on 24 August 1759.

William Wilberforce, although frail in health, became MP for Hull in 1780. Becoming deeply religious, in 1787 he became involved with a society for the suppression of the Slave Trade. Despite threats to his life, in 1797, as well as getting married, he published a book stating that the religious system of the upper classes was against the tenets of true Christianity. The bill for the abolition of the slave trade was finally passed in 1806. Later as MP for Yorkshire he spoke in the debate in 1824 on the abolition of slavery. This bill to abolish slavery in the colonies passed its second reading in July 1833, with Wilberforce dying three days later. The house was opened as a museum and memorial to him in 1906.

The model by Willow Art is a simple grey with a long inscription. It measures 11.3cm wide, 4.5cm deep and 8.5cm high.

C.44755. KNARESBOROUGH: THE OLDEST PHARMACY IN ENGLAND.

KNARESBOROUGH, YORKSHIRE

75 Ye Oldest Chymist's Shoppe in England

Knaresborough dates back to Roman and Saxon times. The castle, overlooking the River Nidd, was built by the Normans in 1100 AD. The town was destroyed by the Scots in 1319, leaving foundations upon which some of the present market-place buildings, including the so-called 'oldest chymist's shoppe,' were built. Although the castle was damaged by Cromwell in the seventeenth century, the nearby buildings remained in good condition.

Legend suggests that a twelfth century underground passage may run between the shop and the castle. However, the present structure, dates to after 1319, with the earliest records of its use as a chemist's shop dating to 1720.

Unusual timber legs support two large shop windows fronting the pavement, above which, set in the red-brick upper structure, are two 'bedroom' windows, with two smaller gable windows above these, one of which is false, possibly as a result of window tax.

The china model, by Carlton, is mainly white, and glazed in various colours on different models with orange, green-blue and brown. It measures 7.7cm wide, 4.2cm deep and 6.6cm high.

LITTLEPORT
CAMBRIDGESHIRE

76 The Transport and General Workers' Union Convalescent Home

In 1855, Canon Edward Bowyer Sparke of Ely Cathedral, vicar of Littleport between 1830-65 and son of the bishop, built the house known as 'The Grange', which was until recently a convalescent home for workers of the TGWU. A subsequent owner, a Mr Peacock, opened a shirt factory in the building to employ the deprived people of Littleport.

During World War I the government requisitioned the property to house Belgian refugees. It was afterwards sold to the London Busmen's Union which in 1922 became part of the TGWU. The new amalgamation turned it into a convalescent home. In World War II, it was a RAF hospital, and reverted again to the TGWU in 1947 when Ernest Bevin was its leader.

It was modernised in 1976, when for the first time wives of members and women members were admitted. In the 1980s it was sold and is now the Grange Nursing Home".

The model by Carlton China is rather unusual in representing a large and complex building with many chimneys and turrets. Details of the building are clearly shown on all four sides and on the top. Its overall measurements are 8.6cm wide, 11.5cm deep and 6.8cm tall.

LONDON

77 The Old Curiosity Shop

The Old Curiosity Shop, near Lincoln's Inn Fields, is a building of unusual shape dating from about 1567 in the reign of Elizabeth I. Today selling curios and bric-a-brac, It has never been rebuilt, although major strengthening operations were undertaken in 1946.

Its fame lies in the fact that it formed the focal point in the novel of the same name by Charles Dickens, but some Dickens experts and historians are sceptical that it is the actual site. Obviously, the original buyers were in little doubt that this was the home of Little Nell, the heroine of Dickens novel highlighting social problems. The tiny bedroom is now used as an office. The model by Willow Art is 8.7cm wide, 3.7cm deep and 6.2cm high

'THE DIAMOND.'

LOUGHGALL, CO. ARMAGH
NORTHERN IRELAND

78 Dan Winter's Cottage

Tradition has it that this cottage, some 200-300 yards from the Diamond Crossroads near Loughgall and Portadown, was the home of Dan Winter and the first meeting place of the group which founded the Orange Order in 1795. As well as the china cottage, the building also features on certain Orange Lodge banners.

At the time when the order was founded Daniel Winter was about 65, a keen Protestant and descendant of Huguenot families from France and England and a 'lapsed' Quaker. Many men were killed at the Battle of the Diamond between the supporters of William of Orange (Protestants) and the Defenders (Roman Catholics) which took place in the fields near the cottage a few days before the first meeting on 21 September 1795.

Dan Winter's descendants moved to a new house nearby in 1953, but the cottage remains and is owned by the Winter family who use it for domestic purposes and as a private museum housing various artefacts. The present Mrs Hilda Winter keeps the fire burning in the old cottage to ensure that it is well aired and that the hidden thatch (now covered with corrugated iron but visible in the model) does not rot.

The unmarked model is quite unlike any others we have seen, apart from President McKinley's (No. 48) to which it is very similar. Both were produced by the Irish Porcelain trade as money boxes and both have glazed white plaques on the front of the model under the doors. This is marked 'Dan Winter's Cottage where the first Orange Lodge was formed in Co. Armagh, Ireland'. It measures 12.8cm wide, 6cm deep and 8.4cm high.

LUDLOW, SHROPSHIRE

79 The Feathers Hotel

THE FEATHERS HOTEL.

The Feathers has been modelled by various companies. That by Willow Art, sometimes also with an ashtray, is 5.4cm wide; 1.9cm deep and 5.6cm high, while the Wilton version measures 8.7cm wide, 4cm deep and 10cm high without a chimney. Both are rather uninspired. In contrast the two produced by an unknown maker (possibly Leadbeater) are among our favourites. One measures 9.3cm wide, 6cm deep and 11.5cm high, with the other slightly larger at 10.7cm wide, 6.6cm deep and 13.2cm high.

Unknown maker

Willow

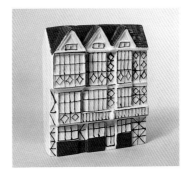

Wilton

This is the most ornate of all the Tudor buildings copied by china model makers. In addition to a great deal of ornamental and carved oak, it has splendid ironwork and a handsome studded door. It dates from at least 1603, and stood within the ancient town walls.

Rees Jones whose initials are on the door leased the property in 1609, before buying it freehold in 1618 and opening it as an Inn.

The first documented reference to the Inn as 'The Feathers' is in a deed of 1656, but it was probably given the name in 1616 when Prince Charles, son of James I, visited the castle. At that time the town was the seat of the Lord President of Wales and the Council of the Marches. Ludlow was the last fortress to succumb to Cromwell in 1646 and the princes lived here before going to London to die.

After a period of decline in the late seventeenth century, Ludlow became fashionable among the local nobility and gentry again in the mid eighteenth century.

**LULLINGTON, ALFRISTON
SUSSEX**

80 Lullington Church

The church, said to be the smallest church in England, dates to the thirteenth century. Its internal dimensions are only 15ft 3ins by 16ft 5ins, but in fact the church at Upleatham, also the subject of a china model (No 89), is slightly smaller. It was originally a chapelry of Alciston Priory first under the control of the Abbot of Battle Abbey and later in 1251 under the Bishop of Chichester, Saint Richard. It may be dedicated either to St Sitha, the patron saint of English housewives, or the martyred Saxon princess St Osyth. The only reference to this is a will of 1521 requesting that a taper be 'sett before Saint Sithe'.

It is surprisingly well proportioned considering that only part of the chancel remains, the nave possibly having been destroyed in Cromwellian times. It was first restored in 1893 and again in 1930. Currently an appeal for £10,000 is in progress in order to deal with dry rot and to reshingle the bell tower.

Services are still held once a month, and, as none are held at Upleathan, this does make Lullington the smallest church in England in use.

The maker of this well-made and well-detailed model is unknown, although Leadbeater is one possibility. It measures 10.4cm wide, 11.6cm deep and 14.2cm high.

**MARKET HARBOROUGH
LEICESTERSHIRE**

81 Old Grammar School

This lovely building was founded in 1614 having been endowed by Robert Smythe who in 1613 gave directions for the 'School House' to be built upon posts or columns over a part of the market place to keep people dry in times of foul weather. He also specified that the dimensions be 36 feet x 18 feet and that certain biblical inscriptions be written upon it. When measured in 1768 it was slightly smaller at 17 feet 6 inches wide. The biblical inscription exists to this day.

Robert Smythe, the son of a poor tailor, left Market Harborough to seek his fortune in London. As a result of his success he became very close to the Lord Mayor and later scholarship boys at the school wore red or black tassells on their mortar boards and City of London Arms on their cricket and football caps.

Lord Mayor's day was celebrated with a bonfire, and fireworks, followed by a sausage and potato supper in the school. The Lord Mayor and Alderman of the City of London were the school governors.

The turret, which contains a small bell inscribed TH 1697, was at one time ornamented with a copper ball and a rich double cross. The floor between the turret and the school chamber housed apartments for the school master's use and until 1869 a staircase entered the school room through the north east corner of the floor. The building was used as a school until 1892.

The models, in two sizes, are by an unknown maker, possibly Leadbeater, and are beautifully coloured. The larger is 12.1cm wide, 7.7cm deep and 15.3cm high, while the smaller measures 10.2cm wide, 6.1cm deep and 13cm high.

MORPETH, NORTHUMBERLAND

82 Morpeth Castle Gatehouse

It is believed that Morpeth Castle was built in the twelfth century, but only the gatehouse remains today. In addition, historical records for the castle are scanty as there was no baron in full time residence after its builders, the de Merlays, left in 1266. Due to its position, the castle and its lands were often in dispute as a result of raids by the Scots. During the Civil War it changed hands several times, before being subject to a full seige which damaged the castle beyond repair.

The Gatehouse was restored in 1858 by the Earl of Carlisle and sold in 1915. Today it is owned by the Landmark Trust who rent it out as a holiday cottage. Inside the vaulted roof of the entrance archway is the outline of a meurtriere (a kind of hole) through which boiling oil could be poured on attackers. There are two angled battlements on which there were tall look-out turrets connected by a gallery.

The heavy, unglazed model is probably by Hewitt & Leadbeater and is one of the largest such models. Despite its size, it is an attractive piece, measuring 12.2cm wide, 10cm deep and 15cm high.

NORFOLK BROADS

83 St Benet's Abbey

All that remains of the Abbey, which was possibly founded on land granted by King Canute in 1020 AD, is an impressive gateway standing at the point on the Norfolk Broads where the rivers Ant and Bure meet. Although small, with rarely more than 25 monks, the monastery was an important one and had many servants and craftsmen. By 1532 discipline among the Benedictine monks was declining and in 1536 the last of the 37 abbots, William Rugge, was appointed Bishop of Norwich by Henry VIII thereby handing over his episcopal properties to Henry VIII. The Act creating the union of the two specified that "the saide monaster of Seynt

Benet" should be maintained and thus this monastery became the only one in England not to have been dissolved. In fact, the abbey was not long kept in service and the last monk left in 1545.

In the eighteenth century, the mill incorporated part of the gateway into its walls. In 1987, a cross of English oak was erected on the place where the high altar would have stood. Today, the Bishop of Norwich, the titular Lord Prior of St Benet's, still visits every year arriving by water.

The coloured model of the abbey by Willow Art measures 4.8cm wide, 3.3cm deep and 4.3cm high. It has been mounted on an ash tray bearing a blue Wroxham crest.

NOTTINGHAM
NOTTINGHAMSHIRE

84 Ye Olde Trip to Jerusalem Inn 1199 AD

Ye Olde Trip to Jerusalem Inn dates to 1199 AD and is reputed to be the oldest in Britain. Said to have been used by crusaders en route to the Holy Land, it originally formed part of the Norman castle's complex of mills, dovecote and brewhouse. Large cellars hewn out of the soft sandstone below add weight to claims that prior to being an inn, it was the castle brewhouse.

The original wooden castle, built by William the Conqueror in 1068 and rebuilt by Henry II in stone, was demolished by Cromwell in 1651. The present castle stands on a post-Conquest site.

The inn, one of the few half-timbered buildings remaining in Nottingham, is now a private residence as well as a public house. It was rebuilt in about 1650. It has a strange ventilator, once a chimney, which opens from the top of a cave beneath the building and ends half-way up the rock face. The pub game known as 'baiting the bull' may have begun here.

The building has been owned by the Ward family for more than 100 years, and it was no doubt they who commissioned the model by Willow Art. It measures 6.4cm wide, 10.8cm deep and 9.6cm high.

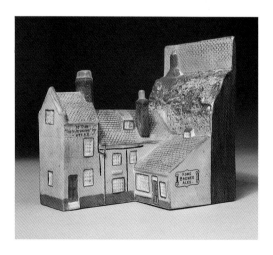

PERTH, SCOTLAND

85 Fair Maid's House

Sir Walter Scott (1771-1832) wrote his novel *The Fair Maid of Perth* in 1828. It was set in the fourteenth century in a house which occupied the site of the present Fair Maids House.

In the novel the beautiful heroine, Catherine Glover, lives with her father, Simon. The Duke of Tothesay, King Robert III's son, tries to abduct her, but is thwarted by Hal O' the Wynd, who marries Catherine and they have a son. Although fiction, much is drawn from the history of the time and local geography. The King, his son and courtiers lived in Perth, a walled city with monasteries protected from the warring clans.

It is not certain when the present house was built, but by 1629 it had been bought by the Glover Incorporation of Perth. A medieval wall which remains part of the interior structure is thought to be the oldest visible wall in Perth.

The Glover Incorporation (Glove Manufacturers etc.) used the building as a meeting hall until the nineteenth century, when it was rented by a cabinet maker for his workshop until 1890. A subsequent owner renovated the building and more importantly enclosed what was an external circular staircase to the right of the main building. In 1899 Perth Town Council purchased the property and it is now a Scottish craft centre.

The house is a beautiful stone building with magnificent heavy shutters and door. A prayer corner in an upstairs room in the present house commemorates the devout and beautiful Catherine.

There are two unmarked models of this cottage. The smaller version has a unique, patchy green roof and measures 8cm wide, 5.5cm deep and 6.6cm high. The larger model, with the open stairs, may be by the same bisque manufacturer of the more common Carnegies Cottage, Dunfermline (No. 65). It measures 8.9cm wide, 7.3cm deep and 8.8cm high and bears the inscription "Fair Maid's House 1860" above the door.

PEVENSEY, NEAR EASTBOURNE SUSSEX

86 Old Mint House

A Norman castle was built in the old Roman town of Pevensey three years after the Battle of Hastings. The old mint house is believed to have been built about 200 years later in 1342. A large, partly timbered building with a red-tiled roof, it stands on the site of a Norman mint which produced coins between 1078 and 1154.

Dr Andrew Borde, King Henry VIII's court physician, owned the house for a time and lived in it during periods when he was banned from the court for indiscretions. King Edward VI, the boy king, stayed here as Borde's guest in 1548, but this relationship did not keep the doctor

from dying in Fleet prison (Debtor's Prison) the following year. The coins which were produced by the Norman mint are all extremely rare. Those of William I and II are nearly all in the British Museum, whilst those of Henry I and Stephen are recorded and very rare indeed.

The property has been intensively commercialised, with entrance fees and a wide range of souvenirs and antiques for sale.

The china cottage, by Willow Art, is marked 'Historical Old Mint House.' It is well designed with much detail, especially on the front windows and in the green ivy or wisteria which covers the tall chimney. It measure 12.3cm long, 4.7cm deep (maximum) and 6.1cm high.

POLPERRO, CORNWALL

87 Couch's House
88 The House on the Props

Polperro, on Cornwall's south-east coast, is a typical fishing village set in a deep and secluded valley with narrow streets and quaint buildings leading down to the creek. Like many Cornish seaside villages it has a tradition of smuggling.

Couch's House was built of the local sedimentary stone and earth (now covered with tallow in lime) late in the sixteenth century. It was occupied in 1800 by William Quiller, a famous privateer and smuggler, whose granddaughter Jane married the multi-talented Jonathon Couch in 1815. Couch (1789-1870) wrote a history of Polperro and a four-volume classic, *History of the Fishes of the British Isles*. He was also a doctor who worked with the mentally retarded. His grandson, Sir Arthur Quiller-Couch, the scholar and writer, never lived in this house. Known as 'the quaintest house in the village', Couch's house was earlier a museum and is now a private residence.

The model by Grafton is very attractive, with white walls, gold windows, a grey-green roof and a tiny fenced garden. It measures 9cm wide, 7.1cm deep and 6.2cm high.

The House on the Props is also said to date from the sixteenth century, but it is more likely to date to between 1800 and 1820. It is remarkable not only for an association with smugglers, but also, for the 15 wooden props supporting its two storeys, which appear to bear the weight of a six foot overhang. The props, from about five feet to eleven feet long, support beams that cross a fulcrum, which in fact bears the weight and are held in place by the main stone wall at one end. The house is now a restaurant, with fanciful beams, ropes and grappling hooks in the style of an old sailing ship. The model, also by Grafton, is 8.9cm wide, 6.3cm deep and (including the width of the bridge, known as Roman Bridge) 10.1cm high.

Left: Couch's House
Right: The House on the Props

RUTHIN CLWYD, WALES

89 Dean Goodman's Birthplace

The model of Exmewe House, St Peter's, Ruthin, carries a caption stating that Dean Gabriel Goodman, who founded Ruthin Grammar School in 1574, was born here on 6th November 1528. The house is named after the family of Sir Thomas Exmewe, a Lord Mayor of London in 1517. In fact the Dean may be said to have re-founded rather than founded the Ruthin school, which may date back as far as 1284 and had certainly been in existence by 1291. The Goodman family owned a second house at the time, Nantclwyd, in Castle Street, and some believe the Dean was born there. Both possible birthplaces still exist. He studied at Cambridge, was associated with the influential Cecil family at Hatfield, and became Dean of Westminster under Henry VIII, when his task was to quell Roman Catholicism and encourage Anglicanism.

The model of the black and white house must have been made by Arcadian either in or before 1921, when it was purchased by Barclays Bank, who modified its appearance. The light grey roof is unusual, since most Tudor buildings were roofed in red. It is 8.9cm wide (overall), 6.3cm deep and 7.6cm high.

SHREWSBURY, SHROPSHIRE

90 Ireland's Mansion

Many of Shrewsbury's historic buildings were tragically knocked down in the name of commercial development during the late 1950s and 1960s. Fortunately Ireland's Mansion was spared and today is much as it was when the model was produced in the early years of this century.

Built in the sixteenth century, it is a large timber-framed building with a red tile roof. Its original owners, the Ireland family, were mercers, or textile dealers, who rented part of the building for monks to use as a carpentry shop. The later, Victorian shop fronts harmonise well with the older timber.

The model is by an unknown maker and is not a particularly fine example. However, as this building and the Ostrich Inn (No. 60) are among the two largest timber-framed buildings modelled in china, we felt it must be included. The measurements are 12.2cm wide, 6.4cm deep and 10.4cm high.

**STOURBRIDGE
WEST MIDLANDS**

91 Dick Whittington Inn

This beautiful Tudor building of oak and wattle daub is said to have been built in 1310 by a rich local landowner, Sir William de Whittenden. It incorporates an even older Gothic arch and has a fine oak staircase as well as Tudor panelling. A secret staircase leading to a concealed room above, and two Jesuit chapels date from Tudor times. There are also two concealed tunnels, one leading to Whittington Hall some 300 yards away, and a second with a fallen roof whose outlet is not known.

Richard 'Dick' Whittington (1358-1423) was not poverty stricken, as the legends suggest, but was the grandson of the wealthy man who had built the inn and the son of Sir William Whittington, who was outlawed because he married a widow without the king's permission. Dick was born in Gloucestershire, the third son of Sir William's second wife. Although there were family estates, he, as only the third son, did not inherit, and went to London where he made his fortune and was elected Lord Mayor of London on four different occasions. He never lived in the inn his grandfather built, but one of its famous residents was Lady Jane Grey, queen for ten days in 1553, who spent some of her childhood here.

The model, one of our favourites, is by Willow Art. It is 10cm wide, 4.1cm deep and 5.9cm high.

STRATFORD-UPON-AVON, WARWICKSHIRE

92 Harvard House

John Harvard was the principal founder of Harvard University at Cambridge, Massachusetts, near Boston. His mother, Katherine Rogers, lived in this house until she married Robert Harvard in 1605. John Harvard was born two years later. He studied at Cambridge, emigrated to America where he was a puritan minister and on his death, in 1638 at only 30, endowed the new college which bears his name with a legacy of nearly £780 (half his estate) and a library of some 300 books.

The house at Stratford, now owned by Harvard University, is a beautiful three-storey building with massive timbers, some elaborately carved. Incised below a first-floor window is 'TR 1596 AR,' the initials of John Harvard's grandparents and the date when they built the house. It is furnished in period and beautifully maintained.

The model is often unmarked, but is to known to be by Willow. Measuring 6.6cm wide, 5.8cm deep and approximately 14.6cm high, the following caption is printed on the back: "1596 The Harvard House, Stratford-on-Avon. Purchased and restored by Miss Marie Corelli for Mr Edward Morris and by him presented to Harvard University, Cambridge, Mass., USA 1909 (to be obtained only from Fred Winter, High Street, Stratford-on-Avon)."

**STRATFORD-UPON-AVON
WARWICKSHIRE**

93 Mason Croft, home of Marie Corelli

Marie Corelli (1855-1924) was a popular and prolific author of romantic and moralistic fiction at the turn of the century writing in all some 28 novels. Unfortunately her style has not withstood the test of time and she is little known today. Marie Corelli was her pseudonym, her real name was Mary Mackay.

Flamboyant, small and aggressive, she was not always tactful, although Queen Victoria and Gladstone, among other eminent people, admired her. She did much to encourage the preservation and restoration of ancient buildings,

including Harvard House (No.92). Advised to leave London for her health, she chose Stratford and after first living in Hall's Croft, William Shakespeare's old home, settled in 1901 in Mason Croft.

Part of the house dates from the seventeenth century, although the majority was probably built between 1735 and 1745, being typical of the symmetrical style of the day.

The models, by Hewitt and Leadbeater, come in three sizes: 7.5cm wide, 4.6cm deep and 7cm high; 9.2cm wide, 5.6cm deep and 8.3cm high; and 10.7cm wide, 6.9cm deep and 10cm high. The front of the model (unlike the house today) is has a green vine, probably Virginia creeper.

**SUTTON COLDFIELD
WEST MIDLANDS**

94 Sutton Park, Druids Well

The 2,400 acre Sutton Park is the largest park in Britain, having resisted various attempts to enclose and divide it.

Druids Well is near Bracebridge pool in Pool Hollies Wood. In 1880 it was described as having a "gothic arched recess, overhung with wild roses, honeysuckle and hollies and surrounded by ferns". The pool was named after Sir Ralph Bracebridge who had constructed the pool in the fifteenth century in order to "ensure a good supply of bream".

The connection with the druids was part of the revival of interest in druids which occurred between the seventeenth and nineteenth centuries. The local Barr Beacon was considered as the seat of the Arch-Druid of England.

It was in 1815 that the Sutton Coldfield Corporation implemented their plan to cover all springs and turn them into wells for the benefit of the local populace. Today, however, such amenities are unnecessary and the Druids Well housing which was some four feet high has been removed to leave an exposed 'well' more reminiscent of a wishing well.

At first sight the model by Willow Art resembles a dog kennel. It bears the Sutton Coldfield crest and measures 6.2cm wide, 4.7cm deep and 4.5cm high.

Bell Hotel, Tewkesbury "John Halifax Gentleman".

Willow

TEWKESBURY
WORCESTERSHIRE

95 The Bell Hotel

This beautiful Tudor building, now a 30 bedroom hotel, may be as early as the sixteenth century, despite the date above the door (1696). It is famous because Dinah Maria Mulock Craik wrote the novel *John Halifax, Gentleman (1856)* while staying there. The hotel features in the book as the home of Abel Fletcher, a wealthy man with a social conscience. John Halifax becomes associated with Abel Fletcher through the latter's invalid son, Phineas Fletcher.

Unknown

Apart from the houses belonging to Shakespeare, Burns and Ann Hathaway, more models seem to have been made of this building by various manufacturers than any other. The only notable exception is that Goss never modelled it.

Willow Art produced three: 5.5cm wide, 2.2cm deep and 5.1cm high; 8.4cm wide, 3.8cm deep and 8cm high; approximately 12.7cm wide, 5.2cm deep and 10.8cm high. The smallest one is also on an ashtray. Arcadian also made a model attached to an ashtray, bearing a Tewkesbury crest: 5.6cm wide, 2.4cm deep and 5.3cm high. The Grafton version measures 8.7cm long, 3.5cm deep and 8.5cm high. Podmore China were reponsible for two versions: the smaller at 7cm long, 3.1cm deep and 6.6cm high; the larger 8.3cm long, 3.8cm deep and 8.5cm high. Finally there is a good large model by an unknown maker measuring 12cm wide, 5cm deep and 10.7cm high.

Podmore

Arcadian

The Guildhall, Thaxted

THAXTED, ESSEX

96 The Guildhall

This marvellous Tudor building was built by the Cutlers' Guild in about 1400, when Thaxted was the centre of the cutlery industry using iron brought from Kent. It was used initially both for guild meetings and as a market place, then when the cutlery trade moved from Thaxted in about the sixteenth century, it fell into disrepair. Eventually it came under the care of a charity, which restored it and turned it into a grammar school. It was given a Georgian roof in 1714, and was considered of such importance that two centuries later the Essex County Council, in 1975, restored it to its original condition as the county's contribution to European Architectural Heritage Year.

The unique shape of the building has been perfectly modelled by Arcadian, smaller at the base than at the top: 6cm wide, 6.7cm deep and 8.3cm high. It is approximately 7.5cm square at roof level.

Trefriw   The Wells.

TREFRIW, GWYNEDD
WALES

97 Trefriw Chalybeate Wells Pump Room and Baths

The waters here were discovered by the Romans in the second century AD. There are two separate springs within a few yards of each other, one having a high concentration of iron and the other of sulphates. The waters were used locally until early in the eighteenth century, when a landslide covered the cave entrance. By 1733, because of a growing fashion for water cures it was excavated and re-opened. A decade later, Lord Willoughby d'Eresby built the first bath house, with a tile floor in the ladies' section, and a mud floor in the mens'.

The pump room, now a private residence was erected in 1873 to dispense waters for drinking,

and, as the demand for bathing grew, baths were installed in the two wings at the rear. It became internationally famous as a centre for curing anaemia, rheumatic disorders, and skin and nervous diseases, and British royalty were among the many visitors. Phials of the water were posted all over the world. By the 1950s the popularity of water cures had declined due to the discovery of penicillin and the building gradually became derelict. The owners began to refurbish the site in 1972, and the ancient cave was reopened in 1977. The waters are now available either there or by post.

The model, unmarked, but possibly Carlton, has colouring on all four sides, but the details are not quite so sharp as in Goss pieces. It measures 8.7cm wide, 9.4cm deep and 8.3cm high.

**UPLEATHAM
CLEVELAND**

98 Upleatham Church

This church competes with Lullington Church in Lullington, near Alfriston (No.80) for the title of smallest church in England. It measures seventeen feet, nine inches, by thirteen feet inside. It has not been a place of worship since 1836 when a larger replacement was built. It was adapted from a small section of a Norman church which had been part of the Guisborough priory until 1640. A tower was added in 1684 – 'William Crow bulded stepel 1684' – to complete the tiny but nicely proportioned building.

By the turn of this century, it had fallen into a ruinous state. Starting in 1923, with funds contributed by, among other sources, the thousands of visitors who came every year, the miniature church was restored. Unfortunately, in recent years, it has again become neglected and vandalised.

Two china models are known, both with details on all sides. The one by Willow Art measures 8.2cm long, 6.2cm deep and 8.6cm high, while the other by an unknown maker, probably Leadbeater is 10.1cm long, 7.7cm deep and 10.3cm high.

WALTHAM ABBEY, ESSEX

99 Waltham Abbey Tower

Waltham Abbey, today near the M25, was on the edge of Epping Forest when it was founded by Harold, Earl of Wessex, later King of England, about the year 1060. The abbey was the last of the monasteries to be destroyed (in 1540) by Henry VIII. The church with its tower on the customary eastern end was saved for the town, although the walls were disintegrating as a result of the razing of the monastery, and in 1552 the tower collapsed.

In 1556 however the present tower was built on the west end as a buttress to stop the rest of the church falling down, thereby conserving a wonderful example of Norman Architecture.

The model is by Willow Art and is of the tower only, measuring 4.5cm square at the base and 10cm high. It was published by W.E. Cuthbert of Waltham Abbey and is extremely rare.

Two views of the same model

WARWICK, WARWICKSHIRE

100 Lord Leycester Hospital

The hospital, or hospice as it was originally called, was founded in 1571 by Robert Dudley, Earl of Leicester, who had been granted a charter by Elizabeth I for this purpose. A corporation consisting of a master and twelve brethren was set up and endowed with an income of £200 per annum.

The hospice was not a new building, but rather a consolidation of a group of existing buildings. The oldest was the ancient chapel of St James, which had been built over the archway of the town's west gate in 1123; of this, only the wall and foundations have survived. The rest of the buildings, erected in 1383 to unite the local guilds, consist of a motley array of gables, fine historic timbering, tiles, stone and brick connected in a piecemeal but appealing way. The Great Hall of St James, which is still used for public functions acquired its name after a banquet held there for King James during a visit in 1617.

The courtyard behind the Great Hall is formed by the Master's House, the Brethren's Kitchen and the Guildhall. The Master's house is the private residence of the Master and was constructed in 1400, while the Brethren's Kitchen was built to provide food for the Chaplains of the Guild. In this room the Brethren cooked and fed communally from the time of the foundation of the hospital until 1950. It is now used for afternoon teas and light refreshments. The Guildhall is used as a small museum for the Hussars.

When the alterations were commenced in 1950, the number of Brethren accommodated was reduced to five temporarily whilst the accommodation was modernised. The buildings were in a dangerous condition due to woodworm and death-watch beetle, and the hospital was not re-opened until 1966 by Queen Elizabeth, The Queen Mother.

The modern flats are lived in by eight ex-servicemen and their wives who give their services towards the running of the hospital in return for their accommodation.

The early model by Willow Art measures 14.6cm long, 5.2cm deep and 9.9cm high, and was published by W H Smith and Co., Warwick.

22171 Wellingborough. Old Houses, Sheep Street.

WELLINGBOROUGH NORTHAMPTONSHIRE

101 Old Tudor House

Among the town's most interesting and historic buildings, these two thatched cottages in Sheep Street are now almost as they were in the seventeenth century. They were restored about 1920 by a Mr Dulley, a local brewer, who intended to open a museum, but instead they became 'The Tudor Restaurant'.

The town itself dates back to Roman times with its name coming from Saxon origins. It was overrun by the Danes when the wooden church was destroyed, but from the ruins a stone church was built and the town prospered to become a busy market town.

The foundations of the Sheep Street houses are said to date from before the year AD 1,000, while the ground floor is thirteenth century and the remainder mainly sixteenth and seventeenth century. The restoration work ensured that as much of the original materials as possible were retained and the only visible difference is that the small gabled window, centre right, was lost.

In the medieval period the buildings had associations with Croyland Abbey and the Old Manor of Croyland. It is alleged that a smiling ghost in grey with a cowl hood haunts the house – possibly a novice monk since monks wore black – but in fact the ghost could date from any time in the last 1,000 years.

In the mid-nineteenth century the buildings housed a flourishing basket-making business. By 1870 one was occupied by Mr Humphries, a broker and auctioneer's clerk. At the turn of the century it was a bric-a-brac shop and was in very bad repair when Mr Dulley took the notion to turn it into a museum.

The beautiful model cottage by Arcadian shows four gabled windows upstairs and is 9.6cm wide, 5.2cm deep and 9.3cm high.

BERMUDA

102 Bermuda Cottage

Bermuda Cottage is a delightful cottage probably by Willow Art, with detail on three sides. Probably on sale in Bermuda around 1920, it is marked 'A Bermuda Cottage' and is typical of cottages on the island with their white stepped roofs, colour-washed walls and the popular green storm shutters, for protection against hurricanes. It was 'Published by S. Nelmes, The Tower, Hamilton, Bermuda' and measures 10.7cm long, 6.3cm deep and 6.4cm high.

WEST YORKSHIRE

103 Red Church

Red Church is typical of the early nineteenth century churches built in West Yorkshire, although we have been unable to locate this model's subject, which may no longer be red and may no longer have clocks on three sides of its tower.

The model is unmarked, but may have been produced by Leadbeater. It measures 15.7cm long, 9.5cm deep (maximum) and 8.9cm high.

MISCELLANEOUS BUILDINGS

Postcript

We hope that you have enjoyed this tour around Britian via miniature coloured cottages. There are just a few which, although not strictly speaking within the scope of our subject, we could not resist including. Castles are an interesting sub-section but would need a separate book to do them justice. Other very attractive models such as the Tumbledown Cottages cannot be located; still others are china rather than porcelain. No doubt when the book is revised additions can be included and we welcome any input from readers.

Aberystwyth University, (Savoy)
Aldburgh, Moot Hall, (unknown)
Beaumaris Castle, Anglesy, (Willow)
Douglas, Isle of Man, Tower of Refuge, (Savoy)
Harlech Castle, (Willow)
Hawarden, The Keep, Near Chester, (unknown)
Hern Bay, Reculver Towers, (Goss)
Luthers Haus, Eisenach, Germany, (unknown)
Monmouth, Monnow Bridge, (unknown and Goss)
Mow Cop, Staffordshire, (unknown)
Newcastle Castle, (Goss)
Nottingham, home of D.H.Lawrence, (unknown)
Oban, Dunollie Castle, (unknown)
Queen's Dolls House, (Cauldon)
Shanklin, Isle of White, The Old Village, (Victis?)
Southampton, Bargate, (Goss)
Tenby, Gateway, (Goss)
Tumbledown Cottage, Unknown location
Tumbledown Cottage with tree, Unknown location, (Savoy)
Wembley, The Stadium, (Crown Ducal)
Windsor Castle, (Willow)
Windsor Round Tower, (Goss)
Worksop, Priory Gate House, (Willow)
    (thought to have been produced coloured)

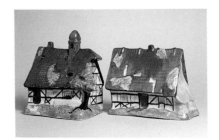

Tumbledown Cottages

Nottingham, home of D.H.Lawrence

Aldburgh, Moot Hall

Harlech Castle

Shanklin, The Old Village

INDEX

Abbey   29, 91, 107
Abbot Reginald   91
Abbot Reginald's Gateway   91
Abbot Reginald's Gateway & Vicarage   67, 68, 91
Abbot Reginald's Wall   91
Abbotsbury   12, 13.
Abbot's kitchen   11, 12, 29
Abell, Jack   41
Aberfoyle   28, 67, 68, 69
Aberystwyth   41
Aberystwyth University   126
Adam   88
Adam, William   77
Admirable Crichton, The   38
Agrostis   37
Alciston Priory   104
Aldeburgh   126
Ale House   14
Alexandria   13
Alfred B. Jones & Sons Ltd   64
Alfred the Great   81
Alfriston   67, 68, 70, 104, 121
Alloway   12, 14, 89
All Saints   91
Alton   67, 68, 71
Alton Towers Amusement Park   71
America   18, 39, 60, 73, 80, 90, 115
American   26, 59, 80
American Colonial   18
Ancient Chapel   36
An Clachan   11, 12, 15, 28
An Clachan cottage   69
Andrew Carnegie's birthplace   65, 67, 68, 90
Anglesey   126
Anglican   25
Anglicanism   112
Anglo/Irish   44
Ann Hathaway's Cottage   11, 12, 55, 63, 64, 65
Ant, River   107
Antrim   67, 73
Arcadian   6, 15, 28, 31, 39, 40, 58, 61, 62, 68-71, 79, 112, 118, 119, 124
Arcadian China   61
Arcadian works   61, 62
Arch Druid of England   117
Arden   5
Arden, Mary   55
Argyll   28
Arkinsall & Sons Ltd   61
Armagh   67, 102
Armour, Jean   14
Arres, Mariota   27
Arthur, King   29
Ashworth, Alice   76
Atlantic   28
Atlantic Hotel   10
Atlantic Ocean   39
Australia   60, 95
Avalon   29
Ayr   7, 12, 14, 65, 67, 68, 72, 89

Baillie, Nicol Jarvie   69
de Balliol, Bernard   74
Ballure   37

Ballymoney   67, 68, 73
Baptist   25
Barclay's Bank   112
Bargate   126
Barnard Castle   67, 68, 74
Barr Beacon   117
Barrie   7, 38
Barrie, Sir James Matthew   38
Battle Abbey   70, 104
Battle of the Boyne   73
Battle of the Diamond   102
Battle of Ledbury   41
Beaumaris Castle   87, 126
Bedgelert   12, 16
Bedford   12, 17, 68
Bedfordshire   17
Bell Hotel   62, 63, 64, 67, 68, 118
Benedictine   107
Benedictine Abbey   67, 125
Bermuda Cottage   67, 68, 125
Bevin, Ernest   100
Bidford   75
Bidford-on-Avon   65, 67, 75
Bird in Hand   35
Birks, Rawlins & Co. Ltd   64
Black Death   86
Blackpool   64, 67, 68, 76
Blackpool & Fleetwood   76
Blackpool Promenade   76
Blagraves, Binkes   74
Blagraves House   74
Blagrove House   67, 68, 74
'Bloody Mary'   27
Board of Trade   46
Boar's Head   74
Boleyn, Ann   53
Bollin, River   48
Bonchurch   65, 67, 68, 77
Bonny, Edward   76
Book of Common Prayer   27
Borde, Dr. Andrew   110
Boston   12, 18, 19
Bourne   67, 68, 78
Bourne-Essendine Railway   78
Bournemouth   7, 12, 20
Bourne United Charities   78
Bracebridge Pool   117
Bracebridge, Sir Ralph   117
Brechin Road   38
Brethren's Kitchen   123
Bridlington   67, 68, 79
Bristol   85
Britain   86, 108, 117
British   39, 59, 80, 120
British Manufacture   65
British Museum   29, 110
Brittany   29
Bronze Age   74
Broom   75
Buckinghamshire   67, 85
Bunyan's Cottage   7, 11, 12, 17, 68
Bunyan, Elizabeth   17
Bunyan, John   7, 17
Bunyan, Mary   17
Bure, River   107
Burns   28, 118
Burns' Cottage   11, 12, 14, 65, 68

Burns' House   67, 68, 89
Burns, Robert   7, 14, 72, 89
Butchers Guild   97
Butchers Lane   97
Butchery   97
Butler, Lady Eleanor   44
Buxton   12, 21, 68

Cain Hall   37
Calais, Governor of   21
Callander   73
Calvin, John   27
Cambridge   9, 18, 112, 115
Cambridge (Mass. USA)   15
Cambridgeshire   67, 100
Cannon St.   62
Canute, King   107
Captain Cook's House   64, 67, 68, 95
Carlisle   31
Carlisle, Earl of   106
Carlyle   96
Carlton   6, 24, 34, 38, 61, 68, 94, 99, 120
Carlton China   61, 63, 64, 100
Carlton Heraldic China   63
Carlton Speciality   63
Carlton Ware   63
Carlton Works   63
Carnegie, Andrew   90
Carnegie's Cottage   109
Carr Dyke   78
Carter's Lane   47
Castle St   112
Cat & Fiddle Inn   11, 12, 21, 68
Catholic Mary   27
Caton la Fidele   21
Cauldon   54, 61, 126
Cauldon Ltd.   9
Cauldon Potteries Ltd   9
Cecil   112
Celtic   87
Chalfont St Giles   67, 68, 79
Chaplains of the Guild   123
Charles, Prince   103
Charles I, King   41, 98
Cheltenham   41
Chepstow   63
Cheshire   4, 8, 67, 86
Chester   126
Chichester   70
Chichester, Bishop of   104
Chinese   47
Christchurch   12, 22, 65, 67, 68, 81
Christian   17, 98
Christians   81
Church   67, 68
Churchill, Winston   14
Church Lands   86
Church of England   29
Church of Scotland   27
Church Stretton   7, 65, 67, 68, 82, 83
City of London Arms   105
Civil War   85, 88, 90, 106
Cleveland   67, 121
Clock Tower   67, 68, 94
Clwyd   12, 44, 67, 112
Coalport China Co. Ltd   9

Coalville   67, 68, 84
Cockermouth   11, 12, 23, 30
Colnbrook   7, 67, 85
Commerce St.   65
Compleat Angler, The   52
Conagher   73
'Concilia'   29
Congleton   65, 67, 68, 86
Conwy   67, 68, 87
Conwy Castle   87
Cook, Captain   95
Cook, James   95
Copeland   8, 10, 57, 58, 61, 68
Copeland, Robert   10
Copyright of cottages   11
Corelli, Marie   7, 10, 19, 115, 116
Cornwall   12, 39, 45, 46, 50, 51, 67, 111
Cornwall, Duke of   46
Cotswold   75
Cottage Pottery   55, 56
Couch, Jonathon   111
Couch's House   64, 67, 68, 111
Council of Marches   103
Craig, Edward Gordon   60
Craigneash   37
Craik, Dinah Maria Mulock   7, 118
Craven Arms   67, 68, 88
Craven, Lord   88
Criccieth   12, 25
Cromwell, Oliver   42, 48, 74, 99, 103, 108
Crown, William   121
Crown Ducal   126
Croyland Abbey   124
Cuthbert, WE   122
Cutlers Guild   119
Cumberland   23
Cumbria   12, 23, 67, 94

Danes   124
Dan Winter's Cottage   67, 102
Dan Winter's Home   68, 73, 102
Darg 'Sandy'   32
Darwin, Charles   96
David Copperfield   77
Davie, John   36
Dawtry, John   53
Dean Goodman's Birthplace   67, 68, 112
Deardon, Sophia   94
Debtors Prison   110
Depression   61
Derbyshire   12, 21
Derbyshire Peak District National Park   71
Dervoch   73
Derwent, River   23
Devon   12, 35, 36, 67, 92
Diamond Crossroads   102
Dickens, Charles   7, 49, 77, 96, 101
Dickens' House   11, 49
Dick Whittington Inn   67, 68, 114
Dictionary of the English Language   43
Digby, Sir Edward   78
Dirleton   32
Dissolution of the Monasteries   86, 91
Dorchester   12, 26

Dorset 12, 13, 26, 47
Dorset Yeomanry 20
Dove Cottage 7, 11, 12, 23, 24, 30
Dove & Olive Bough 23
Douglas 37, 126
Drake-Cutliffe 35
Drewery Place 65
Druid's Well 67, 68, 117
Dublin 43
Dudley, Robert 123
Dugdale, Florence 26
Dulley 124
Dumfries 14, 67, 68, 89
Dundee 72
Dunfermline 65, 67, 68, 90, 109
Dunnollie Castle 126
Durham 67, 74
Dutch 70.

Easby Lane 95
Eastbourne 110
East Dene 77
East Lothian 32
East Lothian District Council 32
Eden Mount 94
Edial Hall 43
Edinburgh 12, 27, 68, 90
Edward I, King 87
Edward VI, King 110
Edward VIII, King 46
Edward the Confessor 92
Eggleston Abbey 74,
Egwin 91
Eisenach 126
Elizabeth I, Queen 101, 123
Elizabeth, the Queen Mother 123
Elizabethan 44, 53
Ellen Terry's Farmhouse 12, 60
Elm St. 62
Elstow 12, 17
Ely Cathedral 100
Empire Exhibition 1938 12, 15, 28, 69
Enchanted Road 34
Endeavour, The 95
England 27, 30, 34, 60, 77, 88, 102, 104,
   107
English 14, 19, 27, 39, 69
English Army 73
English Norman 87
Epping Forest 122
d'Eresby, Lord Willoughby 120
Essex 67, 119, 122
Essex County Council 119
Eoves 91
Eoves-Ham 91
Europe 44
European Architectural Heritage Year
   119
Eve 88
Evesham 65, 67, 68, 91
Exeter 20, 67, 92
Exeter, Bishop of 36
Exeter Cathedral 64, 67, 68, 92
Exeter, Lady 20
Exeter Park Road 20
Exeter Road 20
Exhall 75
Exmewe House 112
Exmewe, Sir Thomas 112

Fair Maid's House 65, 67, 68, 90, 109
Fair Maid of Perth 109

Falcon Pottery 51
Falcon Tavern 75
Falcon Works 8
Far From the Madding Crowd 26
Farley 71
Feathers Hotel 11, 12, 41, 63, 67, 68,
   103
Fenton 63
Filmore, Egerton Jacobson 10
First & Last House 7, 11, 12, 39, 51,
   68
First & Last Post Office 7, 11, 12, 51
First & Last Refreshment House 39
Fisher, Gilbert 78
Fleet Prison 30, 110
Fletcher, Abel 62, 118
Fletcher, Phineas 118
Florence Works 64
Florentine China 64
Ford, Charles 62
Ford, Thomas 62
Forestry Commission 26, 69
Forth, River 69, 90
France 20, 102
Franklin St, No.33 19
Free Church 27
French 27, 85
French Protestant 27
Furnival's Inn 10

Gad's Hill 49
Garrick, David 43
Garrick, Peter 43
Gatehouse 67, 106
Gate House, The 65, 86
Gateway 126
Gelert (the dog) 16
Geneva 27
George V, King 31, 50
George, William 25
Georgian 23, 119
German 44, 65, 90
Germany 9, 126
Gifford, Emma 26
Gladstone, William 96, 116
Glasgow 12, 15, 28, 69
Glass, Andrew 72
Glastonbury 7, 12, 29
Glastonbury Abbey 12
Gloucester 91
Gloucestershire 67, 114
Glover Incorporation 109
Glover, Catherine 109
Glover, Simon 109
Goat Lane 95
Godalming 7, 67, 68, 93
Goodman, Dean Gabriel 112
Goshawk 10, 11
Goss 5-60, 83, 118, 120, 126
Goss, Adolphous 9
Goss China Company Ltd 9, 10
Goss Collectors' Club 54
Goss Cottage Locations 12
Goss England 5, 9, 11, 27, 28, 61, 69
Goss England 'Cottage Pottery' 55, 56
Goss Oven 11, 12, 54
Goss & Peake 8
Goss, Victor Henry 9
Goss, William Henry 6, 8, 9, 10, 29, 54
Goss, William Huntley 9
Goss, W H Ltd 9
Gothic 44, 84, 114

Government School of Design 8
Governor of the Bank of England 19
Grafton 6, 30, 35, 36, 61, 68, 75, 76, 95,
   111, 118
Grafton China 64
Grafton China Works 64
Graham, Douglas 72
Grange Nursing Home 100
Grange-over-Sands 67, 68, 94
Grasmere 12, 23, 30, 68
Gravesend 49
Great Ayton 64, 67, 68, 95
Great Britain 59
Great Expectations 49
Great Hall 87, 123
Great Hall of St. James 123
Great Malvern 67, 68, 96
Great Northern Railway 78
Gretna Green 11, 12, 30, 31, 64, 67, 68,
   96
Guild Hall 67, 68, 119, 123
Guisborough 121
Gullane 12, 32
Gullane Smithy 11, 12, 32
Gunpowder Plot 78
Gwynedd 12, 25, 67, 87, 120
Gynn Inn 64, 67, 68, 76

Haddington 27
Hain, Sir Edward 50
Halfhead 52
Halifax, John 118
Hall, John 55
Hallcroft, John, MP 88
Hal O' the Wind 109
Hallscroft 55, 116
Hamilton 125
Hampshire 12, 20, 22, 53, 67, 81
Hanley 62
Hants, see Hampshire
Hants & Dorset Bus Company 20
Hardy, Thomas 7, 11, 26
Harlech Castle 126
Harley-Jones, A G 63
Harold, Earl of Essex 122
Harold, King 122
Harvard 18, 19
Harvard Glee Club 19
Harvard House 19, 55, 67, 68, 115, 116
Harvard, John 18, 19, 115
Harvard, Robert 115
Harvard University 12, 18, 19, 115
Hastings 34, 110
Hatfield 112
Hathaway, Ann 55, 58, 68, 118
Hathaway, John 55
Hawaii 95
Hawarden 126
Hawarden Castle 87
Headcorn 7, 11, 12, 33, 34
Head, Mr 22
Hebridean 28
H & L, see Hewitt & Leadbeater
Henry II, King 108
Henry VIII, King 53, 79, 107, 110, 112,
   122
Heraldic China 63
Heraldic Ware 63
Hereford 65, 67, 68, 97
Herefordshire 12, 41, 67
Hermitage 45
Hern Bay 126

Hewitt 61
Hewitt, Arthur 65
Hewitt Bros. 61
Hewitt & Leadbeater 55, 58, 61, 65, 68,
   74, 81, 106, 116
Hildyard, R J C 10
Hillborough 75
Higham 49
Higher Bockhampton 12, 26
Highland & Island 28
Historical Old Mint House 110
History of the Fishes of the British Isles
   111
H M Office of Works 13
Holborn 10
Holden, Samuel 19
Holden Chapel 11, 12, 18, 19
Holland 77
Holman, J F 50
Holy Grail 29
Holy Land 108
Hop Kiln 7, 11, 12, 33, 34
Horsham 70
House on the Props 64, 67, 68, 111
Huers House 11, 45
Huguenot 102
Hull 67, 68, 98
Humphries, Mr 124
Hussars 123
Hutchinson, Mary 23

Icknield Way 75
Ilfracombe 10, 12, 35, 36, 50, 64, 68
Industrial Revolution 94
International Exhibition 8
Ireland's Mansion 67, 68, 113
Irene (play) 43
Irish Cottage 65
Irish Porcelain 102
Irving, Sir Henry 60
Isle of Avalon 29
Isle of Man 12, 37, 68, 126
Isle of Wight 65, 67, 68, 77, 126
Italy 45
Ivory Porcelain 63
Izaak Walton's Birthplace 12, 52
Izaak Walton's Cottage 11, 52, 65, 68
Izaak Walton Trust 52

James, Edith 39
James I, King 103, 123
James, H T 39, 40
Jane Grey, Lady 114
Jarman the Innkeeper 85
Jean Macalpine's Inn 28, 67-69
Jerusalem 29
Jesuit 114
Jesus Christ 29
John, King
John Halifax, Gentleman 62, 118
John Knox's House 11, 12, 27, 61, 68
John Milton's Cottage 80
John's Street 8
Johnson, Samuel 7, 43
Johnson's Birthplace 11, 12, 28
Jones, A B 64
Jones McDuffee & Stratton 19
Jones, Rees 103
Joseph of Arimathoea 7, 11, 29
Joseph of Arimathoea, Church of 12,
   29
Jubilee Fund 80

Keep 126
Ken, Ann 52
Ken, Bishop Thomas 52
Kensington China 21, 68
Kent 12, 33, 49, 119
Kent, River 94
Kent Council of Social Services 33
Kerr, James 72
Kilmarnock 14
Kiln of Falcon Pottery 54
Kinnish, John 37
Kirriemuir 12, 38, 68
Knaresborough 67, 68, 99
Knox, John 27
Knox Museum 27

Lake District 23
Lancashire 67, 76
Landmark Trust 7
Land's End 10, 12, 39, 40, 51, 68
Lantern Hill 36, 64
Lantern Room 87
Lawrence, D H 126
Lawrence, D H, home of 126
Laxey 37
Leadbeater 15, 42, 52, 61, 65, 68, 77, 83, 86, 88, 97, 103-105, 121, 125
Leadbeater Art China 58, 61, 65, 82, 88
Leadbeater, Edwin 61, 65
Ledbury 12, 41, 42, 65, 68, 82
Ledbury Market 7, 11, 12, 41
Lee 12, 35, 64
Leicester, Earl of 123
Leicestershire 67, 84, 105
Leith 72
Lewther, Sir James 23
Liberal 25
Lincolnshire 67, 78
Lincoln's Inn Fields 101
Lister, John 98
Litchfield 12, 43
Litchfield Mercury 43
Little Minister, The 38
Little Nell 101
Littleport 67, 68, 100
Little Stretton 65, 67, 83
Lizard, the 39
Llangollen 12, 44, 65, 68
Llanysturndwy 12, 25
Llewelyn, Prince 16
Lloyd George, David 7, 25
Lloyd George's Early Home 11, 12
Lloyd George Museum 25
Lloyd, Richard 25
Lloyd's Bank 97
London 8, 10, 18, 26, 30, 43, 49, 52, 67, 68, 80, 85, 103, 105, 112, 114, 116
London Busmen's Union 100
London Road 8
Long Gallery 86
Longton 63, 64, 65
Look Out House 7, 11, 46, 63, 68
Lord Leycester Hospital 67, 68, 123
Lord Mayor 105, 112, 114
Lord President of Wales 103
Lord Prior of St. Benets 107
Lothian 12
Loughall 67, 68, 102
Lowell, James Russell 18
Lucock, Joshua 23
Ludlow 63, 67, 68, 103

de Ludlow, Lawrence 88
Lullington 65, 67, 104, 121
Lullington Church 11, 67, 68, 104, 121
Luther's Haus 126

Macclesfield 21, 48
Mackay, Mary 116
McGregor, Ellen 69
McKinley, Frank 73
McKinley, James The Trooper 73
McKinley, President 102
McKinley, William 73
Malvern 96
Manchester 25, 94
Manx Cottage 7, 11, 12, 37
Manx Man 37
Market Harborough 65, 67, 68, 105
Market Hall 68, 97
Marram Grass 37
Marriage Act 30
Marriage Room 18
Marston 75
Mary, Queen 31, 53
Mason Croft 55, 67, 68, 116
Maximes Daza, Emperor 13
Melbourne 67, 95
de Merlays 106
'Michael' 23
Middle Ages 85
Milton 69
Milton, John 80
Milton Cottage Trust 80
Milton's Cottage 67, 68, 80
Minister of Edinburgh 27
Moodie St. 90
Moot Hall 126
Monmouth 126
Monnow Bridge 126
Moreton 86
Moreton Hall 86
Moreton Old Hall 67, 68, 86
Morpeth 65, 67, 106
Morpeth Castle Gatehouse 67, 68, 106
Morris, Edward 19, 115
Mosman, James 27
Mount Snowdon 16
Mow Cop 126
Mudeford Run 22
Mystery of Edwin Drood 49

Nanclwyd 112
Napoleon 20, 46
National Trust 16, 24, 26, 60, 86
Naval Officers 46
Nelmes, S 125
Nene, River 78
Nether Bow Theatre 27
Newcastle Castle 126
New England 18
New Foundland 95
New Place 55
Newquay 7, 45, 46, 63, 68
New Quay 45
New World 18
New Zealand 22, 95
Nidd, River 99
Nightingale, Florence 84
Nightlights 18, 19
Nonconformist 17
Norfolk 67
Norfolk Broads 67, 68, 107,
Norman (arch.) 79, 81, 91, 92, 99, 108,

110, 121, 122
Normandy 77
Northampton 12, 59
Northamptonshire 59, 67, 124
Northern Ireland 67, 68, 73, 102
Northumberland 67, 106
North Wales 87
Norwich, Bishop of 107
Nottingham 67, 68, 108, 126
Nottinghamshire 67, 108
Nova Scotia 95

Oak 97
Oban 126
Old Alton 71
Old Betty 80
Old Blacksmith Shop & Marriage Room 30, 31, 67, 68, 96
Old Chapel 36, 64
Old Church 67, 77
Old Court House 11, 12, 22
Old Curiosity Shop 67, 68, 101
Old Falcon Inn 75
Old Falcon Pottery 54
Old Falcon Tavern 65, 67, 68, 75
Old Grammar School 67, 68, 105
Old House 67, 68, 97
Old Left House 22
Old Maid's Cottage 11, 12, 35, 64, 68
Old Manor of Croyland 124
Old Market Hall 7, 67, 68, 82
Old Market House 41, 65
Old Mint House 67, 68, 110
Old Pete 37
Old Pete's Cottage 37
Old Star Inn 67, 68, 70
Old Thatched Cottage 47
Old Thatched Houses 124
Old Toll Bar 12, 30, 31, 64, 68, 96
Old Town Hall 67, 68, 93
Old Tudor House 68, 124
Old Village 126
Orange Lodge 102
Orange Order 102
Ostrich Inn 7, 67, 85, 113
Our Mutual Friend 49
Owen, Robert 25
Oxford 9, 43

Pacific 95
Palace House 53
Palestine 29
Paradise Lost 80
Peacock, Mr 100
Peake, Mr 8
Pebworth 75
Pepper Pot 7, 93
Pepys, Samuel 80
Persia, Shah of 8
Perth 65, 67, 68, 90, 109
Perth Town Council 109
Peter, Dan 38
Pete's Cottage 37, 68
Pevensey 67, 68, 110
Philip of Spain 53
Pilgrim Fathers 18
Pilgrims Progress 17
Pittsburgh (USA) 90
Plant, R H 63
Plant, R H and S L Ltd 63
Plas Mawr 67, 68, 86
Plas Newydd 10-12, 44, 65, 68

Plymouth (Mass.) 18
Podmore 61, 62, 118
Podmore China Co. 62
Poet Laureate 24
Polperro 64, 67, 68, 111
Ponsonby, Sarah 44
Poole 7, 11, 47
Pool Hollies Wood 117
Portadown 102
Portman Lodge 7, 11, 12, 20
Portmeirion Factory 54
Portsmouth 49
President McKinley's Ancestral Home 67, 68, 73
Prestbury 7, 11, 48
Priest's House 7, 11, 48
Prince Llewelyn's House 11, 12, 16
Priory Church 22, 65, 67, 68, 79, 81
Priory Gatehouse 126
Protestant 27, 73, 102
Pugin, A W 84
Pump Room and Baths 65, 120
Pwllheli 25

Quality Street 38
Quaker 102
Quebec 95
Queen's Dolls' house 126
Quiller-Couch, Sir Arthur 111
Quiller, William 111
de Quincey, Thomas 24

R & L see Robinson & Leadbeater
Ramsey 37
Receiver 64
Reculver Towers 126
Redchurch 67, 125
Red Hall 67, 68, 78
Red Lion 28
Return of the Native, The 26
Reverend Rigg 94
Revolutionary 19
Ridgeway & Adderley 9
Riley, Philip 6, 7
Riley, Robin 7
Robert III, King 109
Robin Hood 69
Robinson, Harold Taylor 61, 62
Robinson & Leadbeater 65
Robinson & Sons Ltd, J A 62
Rob Roy 69
Rochester 49
Rogers, Katherine 115
Roman 75, 78, 87, 92, 99, 110, 120, 124
Roman Bridge 111
Roman Catholic 27, 102, 112
Roundheads 42, 48, 80
Round House 67, 68, 70
Royal Doulton 55
Royal Grafton 64
Royalists 41, 80
Royal Mail 41
Royal Mile 27
Royal Shakespeare Theatre 55
Rugge, William 107
Rupert, Prince 41
Ruthin 67, 68, 112
Ruthin Grammar School 112
Rydal Mount 24

Sandwich Islands 95
Sark Bridge 31

Savoy 61, 68, 92
Savoy China 63, 64, 126
Saxon 79, 99, 104, 124
Say 88
School House 105
Scotland 12, 14, 27, 28, 30-32, 38, 67, 69, 72, 89, 90, 96, 109
Scottish Presbyterianism 27
Scott, Sir Walter 69, 109
Sennen 12, 39, 51
Shadow of the Cross 77
Shakespeare's Birthplace 12, 55
Shakespeare's House 11, 58, 63-65, 68
Shakespeare Nightlight 8, 10
Shakespeare, William 55, 60, 62, 68, 75, 116, 118
Shallowford 12, 52, 65, 68
Shamrock 73
Shanklin 126
Shearer, James 72
Sheep Street 124
Shottery 12, 55
Shrewsbury 67, 68, 113
Shrewsbury, Earl of 71, 84
Shropshire 67, 82, 83, 88, 103, 113
Shugborough Museum 52
Silverton 92
du Simitere, Pierre 18
Skye 28
Slave Trade 98
Small Hythe 60
Smythe, Robert 105
Somerset 12, 29
Somerset House 8
Southampton 12, 53, 126
Southey 44
South Wing 86
Spain 45
Sparke, Canon Edward Bowyer 100
Spelman, Sir Henry 29
Spode Museum 10
Stafford 52
Staffordshire 12, 28, 52, 54, 64, 65, 67, 71, 126
Stadium 126
Stars and Stripes 59
Saint Sithe 104
St. Andrews 27
St. Ann 96
St. Ann's Wells 67, 68, 96
St. Bees 94
St. Benet's Abbey 67, 68, 107
St. Bernards Monastery 67, 68, 84
St. Boniface 77
St. Catherine 13
St. Catherine's Chapel 7, 11, 12, 13
St. Ives 7, 11, 12, 50
St. James 123
St. Lawrence 91
St. Michael Square 53
St. Nicholas 7, 36, 50
St. Nicholas Chapel 10, 11, 12, 36, 50, 68
St. Osyth 104
St. Peter 112
St. Richard 70, 104
St. Sitha 104
Stephen 110
Stoke 10, 64
Stoke Corporation 54
Stoke-on-Trent 8, 12, 54, 61, 63, 88
Stokesay Castle Gatehouse 7, 67, 68

Stourbridge 67, 68, 114
Strangeways, Sir Giles 13
Stratford-upon-Avon 12, 19, 55, 67, 68, 75, 115, 116
Stuart 17
Sturgess Street 54
Sulgrave 12, 59
Sulgrave Manor 7, 11, 12, 59
Surrey 67, 93
Sussex 65, 67, 70, 104, 110
Sutton Coldfield 67, 68, 117
Sutton Coldfield Corporation 117
Sutton Park 67, 117
Swan 61, 62
Swan China 62
Swinburne, Algernon 77
Sylvan Pottery Ltd 62
Symes 20

T & C Ford 62
T & G W U Convalescent Home 67, 100
T & G W U 68, 100
Tam o' Shanter Inn 67, 68, 72
Tan House 65, 67, 68, 83
Taylor & Kent 55, 57, 58, 61
Taylor & Kent Ltd 64
Tayside 12, 38
Tehran 8
Tenby 126
Tenterden 12, 60
Terry, Dame Ellen 7, 11, 60
Tewkesbury 62, 63, 67, 68, 118
Thatched Houses in Sheep Street 124
Thaxted 67, 68, 119
Thistle China 15, 68
Thomas, Grace 39
Thomas Hardy's Birthplace 12, 26
Thomas, William 39
Thornton, Sarah 98
Three Old Maid's Cottage 35
Three Old Maids of Lee 35
Times, The 50
Tintern Abbey 63
Titanic 50
Titmus, E M R 29
Toll Bar 11
Tothesay, Duke of 109
Toucan Press 29
Tour of Britain Milk Cycle Race 21
Tower, the 67, 125
Tower of Refuge 126
Town Hall 93
Traditions and Legends of Glastonbury 29
Trappists 84
Treaty of Ghent 59
Treaty of Versailles 25
Trefriw 67, 120
Trefriw Chalybeate Wells 67
Trefriw Wells 10, 65, 68, 120
Tregonwell, Louis 20
Tregonwell Mansion 20
Trinity College 43
Truelock 80
Trumpet of Freedom 25
Tudor 19, 22, 78, 83, 91, 103, 112, 114, 118, 119
Tudor House 11, 12, 53
Tudor Restaurant 124
Tumbledown Cottage 64, 126
Tuscan 46, 61, 68
Tuscan China 63

Tuscan Works 63
Twynham 81

Under the Greenwood Tree 26
Union Jack 59
United Free Church 27
United States 59, 73
Upleatham 65, 67, 104, 121
Upleatham Church 68, 121
USA 12, 18

Vectis 126
Victoria (Australia) 95
Victoria, Queen 80, 96, 116
Victoria & Albert Museum 10
Vine Pottery 64
Virginia 59, 116
Virgin Mary 96
Vivian, Mr 45

W H Smith & Co 123
Wales 12, 25, 29, 44, 67, 112, 120
Wales, north 16, 87
Wales, Prince of 46
Wall, Dr. John 96
Waltham Abbey 67, 68, 122
Walton, Izaak 67
Ward family 108
War of Independence 19, 59
Warwick 67, 68, 123
Warwickshire 12, 55, 67, 75, 115, 116, 123
Washington, George 59
Wedgewood 44
Wellingborough 67, 68, 124
Wellington, Duke of 44
Welsh Border 88
Welsh Office 87
Wembley 126
Wendy House 38
Wessex, King of 81
West Midlands 67, 114, 117
Westminster Abbey 26, 43
Westminster Bank 48, 67
Westminster, Dean of 112
What Every Woman Knows 38
Wheeler, Thomas 97
de Whittenden, Sir William 114
Whittington Hall 114
Whittington Inn 68, 114
Whittington, Richard (Dick) 114
Whittington, Sir William 114
Wilberforce, William 98
Wilberforce, William (Snr) 98
William I, King 110
William II, King 110
William the Conqueror 88, 108
William of Orange 102
Willow 14, 15, 17, 19, 27, 31, 35, 36, 37, 58, 61, 68, 80, 85, 90
Willow Art 6, 15, 27, 31, 36, 55, 61, 65, 78, 83, 84, 85, 88, 89, 90, 93, 96, 98, 101, 103, 107, 108, 110, 114, 115, 117, 118, 121, 126
Willow Art China, Longton 17, 122, 123, 125
Willow China 58, 61
Wilmcote 55
Wilton China 56, 63, 65, 68, 103
Wilton Pottery 63
Wiltshaw & Robinson Ltd 61, 63
Winchester 53

Winchester Cathedral 92
Window in Thrums 11, 12, 38, 68
Windsor Castle 85, 126
Windsor Round Tower 126
Winter, Dan 102
Winter, Fred 115
Winter, Hilda 102
Wixford 75
Wood, Derwent 83
Woodruff, Mr & Mrs 34
Woolworths 47
Worcester 88
Worcester City and County Banking Co. 97
Worcestershire 67, 91, 96, 118
Wordsworth's Birthplace 12
Wordsworth, Dorothy 23
Wordsworth's Home 12, 30, 68
Wordsworth, John 23
Wordsworth, William 7, 23, 24, 44, 84
Worksop 126
World War I 11, 21, 25, 46, 59, 64, 100
World War II 14, 46, 54, 70, 100
Wright, Jimmy 69
Wynne, Robert 87
Yankee 18
Ye Oldest Chymists Shoppe in England 67, 68, 99
Ye Olde 'Trip to Jerusalem' Inn 1199 A.D. 67, 68, 108
Yewbarrow Craggs 94
Yorke, General John 44
Yorkshire 23, 67, 79, 95, 97, 99, 125